The existence of evil, and the huge quantity of it in world history, is probably the most difficult problem in Christian teaching. How can a good and all-powerful God tolerate something so contrary to his own desire? Greg Welty has done an excellent job in replying to this question.... His answer to the problem of evil is the best of all the alternatives. This book is clear, even conversational in its style, but it is a deeply thoughtful, profound analysis. It can be of great philosophical and pastoral help to people who are concerned about this question. I pray that it gains a large readership.

John M. Frame
Emeritus Professor of Systematic Theology & Philosophy,
Reformed Theological Seminary

From his experience as a teacher of philosophy, Greg Welty has distilled a clear, balanced, modest treatment of God and evil. His argument is that God permits evil for a greater good. The author does justice both to divine sovereignty and to the reality of human evil. Though he is an expert philosopher Greg has written here for the general reader. He keeps clear of jargon, making the book widely accessible. It will engage those who have long been perplexed by evil in God's world, as well as those approaching the issue for the first tim

Paul Helm

Eme  sophy of Religion,
; College, London

Is it possible to provide a justification for God's role in the problem of evil by appealing to a greater good? Greg Welty thinks so and mounts a very accessible and clear case for its rationale. When the sovereignty of God is properly coupled with his inscrutability, the necessity of evil so that good may come, says Welty, takes its proper place. Unlike most proposed solutions to this problem, Welty refuses to sacrifice God's meticulous sovereignty at the altar of man's autonomous choices. This book will have to be taken seriously by all who see the problem of evil as a stranglehold on Christian truth.

K. Scott Oliphint
Professor of Apologetics and Systematic Theology,
Westminster Theological Seminary

This is a book I've desperately wanted someone to write for years. It tackles what is arguably the preeminent challenge to the truth of Christianity—the problem of evil—and does so with clarity, profundity and faithfulness to God's word. Deep enough for philosophers and accessible enough for the person in the pew, this volume provides much-needed reassurance that God really does work all things for good.

Michael J. Kruger
President and Samuel C. Patterson
Professor of New Testament and Early Christianity,
Reformed Theological Seminary

This is a very well written book that addresses a perennial question, the question of theodicy, a question that is not easy to answer. Welty tackles the question well with balance, biblical faithfulness, and helpful insights as he makes the 'Greater Good argument.' I was personally edified by this work and I am glad to commend it.

Daniel L. Akin

President of Southeastern Baptist Theological Seminary

Clear, logical, precise, and yet accessible, this book is a superb resource to put in the hands of those troubled by the question, 'How can there be an all-good, all-powerful God, given all the world's evils?' Welty does not, as so many Christian 'answers' to this question tend to do, offer nonbiblical explanations for our world's pain and suffering. He gives Scripture's response which, as his final chapter on objections to his approach makes clear, is ultimately the best response.

Mark R. Talbot

Professor of Philosophy, Wheaton College

Greg Welty has written the book I'd always wanted to read on the problem of evil. First and foremost, he is faithful to the Biblical witness. Secondly, he is gentle and sensitive as he pursues the problem. Thirdly, he has a rapier-sharp mind with which he parries the atheist's thrusts and deftly turns aside the attack. Finally, he knows where to stop. Many Christians over the years have overreached themselves by saying that they have the final answer to settle the problem once and for all. Welty, by contrast, is careful not to go further than God's revelation in the Bible allows him to— but he is also careful to explain why we should be satisfied with that. Well written and readable, this book should be of interest and benefit to believer and atheist alike.

Daniel Hill

Senior Lecturer in Philosophy, University of Liverpool

The greatest strength of this book is that it answers the philosophical question concerning the problem of evil with thoroughly biblical answers. Dr. Welty has a unique grasp both of philosophical arguments and biblical exegesis. He ably anticipates and answers philosophical objections to the biblical teaching that our all-knowing and all-wise God sovereignly brings about a greater good through the evil he allows. He also explains the various kinds of goods God brings out of both human sin and natural calamities. Dr. Welty doesn't duck the hard questions, but answers them in a way that ordinary Christians can understand and then apply in their discussions with unbelievers. Among the most helpful features of this book are the succinct summaries at the end of each chapter, the numerous biblical examples, and the practical illustrations which help to make abstract concepts concrete.

Jim Newheiser
Director of the Christian Counseling Program
Associate Professor of Counseling and Practical Theology,
Reformed Theological Seminary

Oh no, I thought, *not another small book on the problem of evil*. But because 'the problem' of evil is the number one reason for non-belief I hear from non-Christians and is something I think about continually, I read on! And I'm glad I did. This is a small but brilliant book on the whole subject. It is not trite nor shallow. It does not offer a general 'off the shelf' theodicy which you can give to your friends. But it will really help the thinking Christian to see that evil is a greater problem for the non-believer as well as being a great opportunity for the believer to proclaim the goodness and glory of the God who delivers us from evil. This is serious work and seriously outstanding. Highly recommended!

David Robertson
Minister, St Peter's Free Church, Dundee

This is precisely the sort of book we need today. With clarity and concision, Greg Welty provides a penetrating look at the existence of good and evil in the world, the harsh reality of sin and suffering in our lives, and the role of our righteous, loving, and sovereign God over all. Whether you are a Christian or sceptic of Christianity, this book is sure to aid you.

Burk Parsons
Co-pastor of Saint Andrew's Chapel, Sanford, Florida
Teaching fellow at Ligonier Ministries

Christian theology should always lead us to worship. It should humble us and remind us that God is the Creator and we are but His creatures. Dr. Welty's *Why is There Evil in the World?* wrestles with one of the deep mysteries of our faith, recognizing our own limitations and calling us to bow down before our sovereign Lord. Reading this book will cause you to think deeply and to worship reverently.

James M. Renihan
President of IRBS Theological Seminary

THE BIG TEN
Critical Questions Answered

SERIES EDITORS
James N. Anderson and Greg Welty

Why is There Evil in the World (and so Much of It)?

Greg **Welty**

Scripture quotations are from *The Holy Bible, English Standard Version*, copyright © 2001 by Crossway Bibles, a publishing ministry of Good News Publishers. Used by permission. All rights reserved. ESV Text Edition: 2011.

paperback ISBN 978-1-5271-0141-8
epub ISBN 978-1-5271-0204-0
mobi ISBN 978-1-5271-0205-7

Published in 2018
by
Christian Focus Publications Ltd,
Geanies House, Fearn, Ross-shire
IV20 1TW, Scotland
www.christianfocus.com

Cover design by Paul Lewis

Printed and bound by
Bell & Bain, Glasgow

CONTENTS

Preface

The problem of evil is one of the most challenging objections to the Christian faith, a faith which insists that a perfectly good God exists despite the pain and suffering in the world. It is also one of the most discussed objections, and books like this (large or small) are legion. When writing books on the problem of evil, Christians often face a tension between simply *stating what the Bible says* about God's relation to evil, and *offering philosophical reasoning* that goes far beyond the text of the Bible. On the one hand, how can a mere statement of biblical teaching help with the problem of evil? Doesn't the biblical teaching *generate* the problem of evil in the minds of many thoughtful inquirers (including you who are reading this book right now)? Isn't the fact that the Bible presents a God who is powerful enough, knowledgeable enough, and good enough to get rid of all evil, something that makes the evil in the world a reason to *reject* such a God? On this view, the Bible could only confirm for us that the critics are right, by supplying us with the very premises of the problem of evil! On the other hand, if we solve the problem of evil by offering philosophical reasoning not found in the Bible, aren't we admitting that the Bible 'isn't enough'? Aren't we saying that God left his people for at least two millennia now without a solution to this problem, but if we would only listen to a bunch of really clever folks, we might be able to solve what the Bible cannot solve? So on the one hand the biblical teaching is irrelevant as a solution, and on the other it is insufficient.

In my view this is a double mistake. First, Christians are *already* committed to the entire truth of the Bible. They cannot run away from its teaching about God, the world, and God's relation to it. It would be foolish for Christians to hide the teachings of the Bible from those who are skeptical about the truth of the Christian faith, in order to ultimately persuade them to embrace the teachings of the Bible. Far better to make clear the Christian point of view at the outset, for (as I will argue throughout this book) there are fundamental themes in the Bible—often neglected in these discussions—which *when taken together* point towards a powerful solution to the problem of evil. If we consider any of these biblical themes in isolation from each other, it might be quite easy to persist in thinking that evil is an argument against God's existence. But put together they provide very good reason to resist the conclusion that the evil in the world makes it unacceptable to believe in God. Thus, stating the biblical teaching whenever relevant can never hinder but only help. Second, having studied the problem of evil as a philosopher of religion for quite a few years, it seems to me that the best philosophical reasoning available on the subject helps to confirm what Christians already claim to know on the basis of the Bible. So the role of philosophy can be to complement and confirm the Christian message. Such reasoning, though not found in the Bible, can be used to defend the biblical teaching from various spurious objections, by clarifying what the alternatives really are, and by bringing to light unwarranted assumptions that are often presented by critics as eminently reasonable but in reality are anything but that. This is a useful role for philosophy to have, and I hope it plays such a role in this book.

In the first chapter I state concisely what the 'problem of evil' is supposed to be: an argument against the existence of God that starts from the pain and suffering in the world and concludes that this pain and suffering make the existence of God very unlikely, if not impossible. I go on to offer definitions and draw distinctions that will be helpful in clarifying not only what this problem is supposed to be, but what any plausible solutions will have to look like.

Then in the second chapter I state what I take to be the best solution to the problem of evil, and I try to motivate that solution both biblically and philosophically. In summary, the pain and suffering in God's world play a necessary role in bringing about greater goods that could not be brought about except for the presence of that pain and suffering. The world would be worse off without that pain and suffering, and so God is justified in pursuing the good by these means. I go on to emphasize in chapters three and four some themes that enhance the viability of this 'Greater-Good' approach: divine sovereignty and divine inscrutability. God ordains whatsoever comes to pass, both good and evil (so, divine sovereignty). But *how* a specific evil contributes to and is outweighed by a greater good in the plan of God is typically not discernible by us (so, divine inscrutability). My solution is therefore a 'theodicy' in that it attempts to justify (Greek: *dike*) the ways of God (Greek: *theos*) to men in the face of widespread pain and suffering that strikes us as wholly *un*justified.

So the first four chapters of this book give a positive statement of both the problem of evil and the theodicy that is best equipped to solve it. Undoubtedly my positive presentation will raise questions in readers' minds. What about all of the *other* things Christians have said in response to the problem of evil, things that are very different from what I say in chapters two through four? Is any of that of value, and why? So in chapter five I consider whether free will or the laws of nature could be appealed to as a solution to the problem of evil. Finally, how can the Greater-Good theodicy be defended from the battery of accusations typically raised against it? My handling of these various objections occurs in the final, sixth chapter of the book.

In applying the twin themes of divine sovereignty and divine inscrutability, I develop and extend their application in a way that brings other kinds of theodicy to bear upon the problem. (I regard the Greater-Good theodicy as a kind of 'umbrella' approach that can incorporate important insights to be found in other traditional theodicies.) My main point throughout will be that although we as humans may not know enough to 'rule in' a theodicy as explaining a particular evil on a particular occasion, the burden of proof is on the critic of Christianity to show that we know enough to *rule out* the applicability of the available theodicies. In the very nature of the case I don't think this burden can be met, and so I don't think the 'problem of evil' can ever be an *intellectually rational* reason to reject the existence of God. Or so I will argue.

From time to time I refer to specific books and authors, each of which can be easily found through a simple internet search if the reader so wishes. This frees me from interrupting the reader with an apparatus of textual notes. Bible references such as 'John 17:24' refer to the Bible book called 'John,' to the seventeenth chapter of that Bible book, and specifically to the twenty-fourth verse of that chapter. Thus, 'book name xx:yy' refers to chapter xx, verse yy of book name. Most versions of the Bible have a table of contents with page numbers to help you locate each book by name. When I cite the Bible, my quotations will be from the English Standard Version, available at *www.esvbible.org* for free. All italics in biblical quotations are my own.

1

What is the Problem of Evil?

ASKING QUESTIONS VS. PROPOSING AN ARGUMENT

The problem of evil typically starts with questions, indeed with some of our most heartfelt inquiries about the world and God's relation to it. 'Why does God permit evil and suffering?' 'Why doesn't God prevent this evil in particular?' Christians are routinely challenged by others who pose these sorts of questions, and yet sometimes it's hard to know where the 'problem' really lies. After all, a Christian *could* say, 'Well, I don't know the answers to your questions. Is there a problem with that? There are lots of things we Christians don't know. I don't know the exact year King David was born. I don't know why God called Abraham out of Chaldea, rather than his brother Nahor. Does my ignorance on these and many other points mean Christianity is false? Why would that follow?'

Such a reply seems flippant, even though a good point is being made: mere questions are not arguments! But this case seems different, because usually when *these* questions are asked—questions about why God doesn't prevent evil—there is an implicit *argument* against Christianity going on beneath the surface. Standing behind the question is something like the following line of reasoning: 'Well, if you can't give me a reason why God permits this evil, then there probably *isn't* a reason! After all, aren't you Christians supposed to be in the know about these sorts of things? And if there isn't a reason that justifies God in any way, one that absolves him from blame, then a perfectly good God doesn't exist.'

So although we should distinguish between merely asking questions about evil and proposing an argument against God from evil, charity should lead us to conclude that most thoughtful inquirers on this subject are pursuing *a line of reasoning* that ends with the nonexistence of God. That reasoning may be implicit, undeveloped, and sometimes mixed in with anger or bitterness, but it is there. The reasoning needs to be stated explicitly so that its underlying assumptions can be examined and criticized, and it is this kind of approach that is taken in this book. Towards this end, I assume that a burden rests upon *both* sides, both upon those making the argument (the critic, the disbeliever in God) and those to whom the argument is directed (the

Christian, the believer in God). *On the one hand, the critic's burden is the burden of proof.* He who affirms must prove. If the critic of God's existence thinks that the existence of evil is evidence against or even disproof of God's existence, *then the critic must make an argument.* He cannot rest content with asking puzzling questions. Of course, many critics have made an argument, and we shall examine one or two of them shortly. *On the other hand, the Christian's burden is the burden of response.* If the critic of God's existence *has* made an argument, then it is incumbent on the Christian to say *something* in response (rather than avoid unbelievers or merely pray for them). This is simple Christian duty, not to mention witness, and there are explicit biblical texts about this. 'But in your hearts honor Christ the Lord as holy, always being prepared to make a defense to anyone who asks you for a reason for the hope that is in you; yet do it with gentleness and respect' (1 Pet. 3:15). 'Walk in wisdom toward outsiders, making the best use of the time. Let your speech always be gracious, seasoned with salt, so that you may know how you ought to answer each person' (Col. 4:5-6). Jesus himself took the time to listen to and then relevantly respond to the arguments of those who were opposed to his beliefs, and we see an extended account of this in Luke 20:27–40.

Hume's and Epicurus's statement of the problem of evil

David Hume, the eighteenth-century Scotsman and Enlightenment skeptic of religious doctrine, has been an important influence on the contemporary discussion of 'the problem of evil.' In Part X of his *Dialogues Concerning Natural Religion* (1779), Hume argues quite forcefully that

> the pain and suffering in the world is not, by any means, what we expect from infinite power, infinite wisdom, and infinite goodness. Why is there any misery at all in the world? Not by chance, surely. From some cause then. Is it from the intention of the Deity? But he is perfectly benevolent. Is it contrary to his intention? But he is almighty. Nothing can shake the solidity of this reasoning, so short, so clear, so decisive....

In Hume's view, pain and suffering are not what we would *expect* to see in a world governed by the infinity of divine power, wisdom, and goodness. God's power means he *could* prevent any pain and suffering, his wisdom means he would *know how* to prevent it, and his goodness means that he would *want* to prevent it. So there should be no pain and suffering. But there is! It follows that the God whose existence *would surely* have prevented all this pain and suffering simply does not exist.

Hume's reasoning not only echoes but is arguably derived from that of the ancient Greek philosopher Epicurus (fourth century B.C.), whose argument was preserved in the writings of the Christian apologist Lactantius (third century A.D.): 'Is God willing to prevent evil, but not able? Then he is not omnipotent. Is he able, but not willing? Then he is malevolent. Is he both able and willing? Then whence cometh evil? Is he neither able nor willing? Then why call him God?' These four questions elegantly communicate the concerns of many who have struggled with the problem of evil. Indeed, they may communicate *your* concerns as you read this book, in your quest to see if Christians have anything sensible to say on this topic!

So what is the argument, exactly?

An argument is a series of claims that are made in support of another claim. The series of claims are the assumptions or 'premises,' and the claim that gets supported by them is the 'conclusion.' If an argument is a good one, then it not only has premises that strike the reader as highly likely to be true, but those premises do in fact support the conclusion (rather than being irrelevant to it). The premises are the argument's content and the way the conclusion is supported by the premises is the argument's structure. This means that there are ever and always two fundamental ways to respond to any argument: challenge its content (maybe the premises aren't *true*), or challenge its structure (maybe the premises, true or not, don't *support* the conclusion).

Epicurus's problem of evil can be spelled out so that we can see its content and structure at a glance. His argument consists of four claims:

Epicurus's words	My paraphrase of Epicurus's words
'Is God willing to prevent evil, but not able? Then he is not omnipotent.'	1. A perfectly powerful being *can* prevent any evil.
'Is he able, but not willing? Then he is malevolent.'	2. A perfectly good being *will* prevent evil as far as he can.
'Is he neither able nor willing? Then why call him God?'	3. God is perfectly powerful and good.
'Is he both able and willing? Then whence cometh evil?'	4. Therefore, if a perfectly powerful and good God exists, then there is no evil.

The significance of the conclusion is obvious: since there *is* evil, a perfectly powerful and good God doesn't exist. Notice that this conclusion depends on recognizing two key attributes of God (premise 3), and on claiming that each of these attributes implies something about evil in the world (premises 1 and 2).

DEFINING 'EVIL' AS 'ANY SIGNIFICANT CASE OF PAIN AND SUFFERING'

The above argument talks a lot about 'evil,' and concludes that the existence of evil is incompatible with the existence of God. But what is 'evil'? On some definitions, maybe evil is some strange, quasi-ethereal substance: there is the physical event of the mugger stabbing his victim in the dark alleyway, and this is an event we can see, but maybe 'evil' is some sort of *judgment* we make about this event, some invisible norm or standard we attach to that action, so that 'evil' is really something over and above that physical event, maybe even something in our heads, something we make up, something relative to societies and cultures. If so, perhaps we have a quick way out of the problem of evil. There is no evil! There are just the things that happen in the world (those are real), and then there are our judgments about those things (we judge they're bad), but those judgments are up to us and could be wrong. And surely God doesn't fail to exist simply because we happen to call certain things 'evil'! So the problem of evil is an utter failure, and having dispensed so quickly with the problem, this book should really stop here and be reissued as a pamphlet.

Clearly something has gone drastically wrong. This interpretation of 'evil' as a subjective, mental non-entity is not one that any serious *advocate* of the problem of evil accepts, nor is it the conception of evil that *Christian respondents* to the problem have ever accepted! The problem ought never to be trivialized in this way. What generates the problem of evil for so many thoughtful inquirers is the enormous amount of *pain and suffering* in the world: that brought about by rapists and racists, by mass shooters and malevolent dictators, by tsunami and swindlers, by car wrecks and cancer and child abuse. The problem of evil can be stated by referring to all this pain and suffering, and arguing that a powerful God *should* prevent it, a good God *would* prevent it, and so its existence testifies to the nonexistence of God. The fact that pain and suffering exist doesn't depend in any way on our subjective judgment about it. Suffering is painful regardless of what we think.

Go back to the Epicurean problem of evil stated above. Replace every occurrence of the word 'evil' with the phrase 'significant case of pain and suffering.' The argument seems as powerful as ever. For any significant case of pain and suffering in the world, it certainly seems as if a being as powerful as God *could* easily prevent it. If a lowly superhero like Superman could easily break the bones of the rapists, punch racists into the next century, use his laser eyes to melt the shooters' guns, (literally) throw any dictators into jail, catch school buses that fall off bridges, and so on, then surely the all-powerful God of the Bible can prevent *any* case of pain and suffering in the world. He brought the very world into existence; what mishap could he not prevent?

And for any significant case of pain and suffering in the world, it certainly seems as if a being as good as God *would* want to prevent it. Don't *we* want to prevent the things on my list? We're not all that good ourselves, but that doesn't stop us from banding together to eradicate crime, to convict dictators in international courts, to promote road safety, and so on. Isn't God at least as good as that? Jesus seems to think so, for in one of his most famous sermons—the Sermon on the Mount—he says: 'If you then, who are evil, know how to give good gifts to your children, how much more will your Father who is in heaven give good things to those who ask him!' (Matt. 7:11). If *we* seek to promote the good and prevent the evil, at least much of the time, how much more would a perfectly good God!

So the terms 'powerful' and 'good' in the above argument mean something. They mean that a powerful person can prevent pain and suffering (and a perfectly powerful person can prevent it all), and that a good person would want to prevent pain and suffering (and a perfectly good person would seemingly want to prevent it all). If God's power doesn't give him the means to prevent suffering, and if God's goodness doesn't give him any motivation to do so, then he is not powerful or good in any recognizable sense of these terms. And in that case the conclusion of the problem of evil would be true: there really is no God.

So for the remainder of this book, 'evil' will be defined as 'any significant case of pain or suffering.' The problem of evil is a challenge to the existence of God precisely because the pain and suffering in the world seem to conflict with what a perfectly powerful and good being would permit.

TESTING OUR DEFINITIONS: THE 'YOU CAN'T DEFINE EVIL' RETORT

The thoughtful skeptic of God's existence who is reading this book may be interested to know that defining 'evil' as 'any significant case of pain and suffering' grants an advantage to the skeptic, protecting the critic of God's existence from a retort that is often on the lips of Christians: 'Well, you're not a Christian or a believer in God, so you reject God's norms for life. In fact, you have no way of justifying or explaining or knowing the difference between good and evil! But if you can't even *define* "evil," then you can't raise a "problem of evil" for us Christians. And if you can't raise the problem, there is no problem.' As a professor in a Christian seminary I often hear this retort from well-meaning students. (Perhaps it's a bid to quickly dissolve the problem and make my lectures shorter, thereby killing two birds with one stone!)

Christians who argue in this way are mistaken, and that for two reasons. First, *even if* unbelievers have no way of defining 'evil' (because they lack belief in God and his standards), the fact remains that *Christians* think there is such a thing as evil. And what the problem of evil says is that there is a conflict between the existence of evil things *as Christians define 'evil'* (say, breaches of the Ten Commandments) and the existence of God *as Christians define him*. This is an apparent contradiction within the Christian view of the world, and the problem of evil is making this contradiction apparent. The skeptic doesn't have to supply any definitions of his own; he can start with the Christian's convictions. Why would God allow so much breaking of his holy law, when he could prevent it and he would want to prevent it? The problem of evil can therefore start from *Christian assumptions* about evil and God, rather than from the skeptic's assumptions, and go from there. (Don't Christians regularly argue that atheists are contradictory about something or other? Well, the problem of evil is the atheist returning the favor.)

Second, even if skeptics cannot justify moral standards, it is still true that the words which Christians use to describe God have a particular meaning. And surely it is part of the meaning of 'good' that a good person has to have *some* motivation to prevent pain and suffering. If someone douses a German shepherd dog with gasoline and then sets it on fire in my presence, and I just stand there doing nothing, just permitting it for the fun of it, I can scarcely call myself 'good'. This is what critics of God's existence are saying in the problem of evil: how can God be 'good' if he permits enormous amounts of pain and suffering that he could easily prevent? Thus, defining 'evil' as 'any significant case of pain or suffering' wards off a red herring in the debate over the problem of evil: the dubious notion that if the critic doesn't believe in or can't define objective evil then he can't justifiably raise a problem of evil for the Christian.

DISTINGUISHING BETWEEN TWO KINDS OF EVIL (MORAL AND NATURAL)

There is a vast amount of significant pain and suffering in the world. Those who argue against God's existence from this evil, and those who defend God's existence in the face of this evil, have found it useful to distinguish between two kinds of evil: moral evil and natural evil. The importance of the distinction will only become clear later in this book. But to summarize, some skeptics think that by focusing on a particular kind of evil, they can construct a more powerful version of the problem of evil. And some Christians think that by telling one type of story on God's behalf (a 'theodicy') they can explain one kind of evil, and by telling another type of story they can explain the other kind of evil. So as a means of clarifying the debate to come, let's make this distinction clear.

The first kind of evil is 'moral evil.' Moral evil is any evil—that is, any significant case of pain and suffering—which is caused by free persons, either intentionally or through culpable neglect of their responsibilities. Christians sometimes call these 'sins of commission' and 'sins of omission.' It is doing what ought not to be done, and leaving undone what ought to be done, such that the consequence is lots of pain and suffering.

So, moral evils are things like murder, adultery, rape, theft, racism, exploitation, verbal abuse, and so on. In these cases, people are intentionally and deliberately inflicting pain and suffering on each other. And the suffering doesn't have to be restricted to that of *humans*. Many advocates of the problem of evil emphasize the problem of *animals* suffering needlessly at the hands of humans. (I described a vivid case of animal abuse at the end of the previous section.)

Many more cases of moral evil occur through culpable neglect. If I'm sitting by a swimming pool reading my tablet and I see a toddler go by and topple into the pool, then flail its arms around helplessly, then start gurgling as it drowns—and I do absolutely nothing when it is in my power to act—I have neglected my responsibilities in this situation, and I am guilty of adding to the moral evil in the world. It was up to me whether I prevented this pain and suffering, and I didn't prevent it. One might even go so far as to say I partially caused it, since causes are what 'make a difference' in the course of events from what they would otherwise be, and my neglect made a difference as to the pain and suffering in the world. A large proportion of moral evil is of this type.

The second kind of evil is 'natural evil.' Natural evil is any evil that is not moral evil. It is significant pain and suffering in the world that are *not* caused by free persons either intentionally or through culpable neglect of their responsibilities. Where does it come from, then? For lack of a better term, from 'how nature goes on,' quite independently of human choices. Natural evil is evil caused by impersonal objects and forces, rather than by the choices of persons. So, natural evils are the pain and suffering that come in the wake of things like tornados, hurricanes, earthquakes, tsunamis, (naturally-occurring) plague and disease, (most) genetic defects, (most) forest fires, falling trees, the rampaging of savage animals, and so on. (The qualifications of 'naturally-occurring' and 'most' are needed because at least some plagues, diseases, genetic defects, and forest fires can arise through scheming humans, in which case they are moral not natural evil.)

Christians (and insurance policies!) sometimes call natural evil 'acts of God,' but that is typically to convey the idea that the evil in question was beyond the intention or control of the human persons on the scene. The point of the terminology is to say it wasn't an 'act of humans.' In any event, no one says, 'I hate you, and I'm sending a tornado your way right now!' We can't cause these kinds of suffering by our choices. Rather, tornados are natural evils because there is, broadly speaking, a scientific explanation of them in terms of a natural state or condition at the time and the laws of nature which describe what happens in those circumstances due to forces and objects in the vicinity.

None of that involves explaining the pain and suffering with reference to human intentions or choices, and so we have what is essential to natural evil. And again, many natural evils involve the pain and suffering of animals, such as those which are grievously burned in naturally-occurring forest fires. This widens the scope for natural evil considerably.

Thus, in the remainder of this book, 'evil' will be referring to these two kinds of pain and suffering: one kind brought about by human beings choosing to inflict pain and suffering on each other (or culpably failing to prevent it), and the other kind brought about in virtue of 'how nature goes on,' regardless of human choices.

DISTINGUISHING BETWEEN TWO KINDS OF RESPONSE TO THE PROBLEM OF EVIL

Should Christians attack the content of the argument, or its structure instead? I said earlier that there are two ways to attack an argument: its content and its structure. Either there is something wrong in the assumptions of the argument (the premises aren't true), or there is something wrong in its structure (the premises don't support the conclusion). In order not to waste the reader's time, I earlier presented a version of the problem of evil (inspired by Epicurus) that seems impeccable in its structure. That is, *if* the premises are true, then the conclusion *must* be true, because in this case the premises not only support the conclusion, they *require* it. Here is the argument again:

Epicurus's words	My paraphrase of Epicurus's words
'Is God willing to prevent evil, but not able? Then he is not omnipotent.'	1. A perfectly powerful being *can* prevent any evil.
'Is he able, but not willing? Then he is malevolent.'	2. A perfectly good being *will* prevent evil as far as he can.
'Is he neither able nor willing? Then why call him God?'	3. God is perfectly powerful and good.
'Is he both able and willing? Then whence cometh evil?'	4. Therefore, if a perfectly powerful and good God exists, then there is no evil.

The logical structure of the argument is 'tight'—if you have good reason to accept the premises (claims 1, 2, and 3) then you have good reason to accept the conclusion (claim 4). In short, if God's power *can* prevent any evil and God's goodness *will* lead him to prevent any evil his power can prevent, then if God exists *all evils will in fact be prevented*. Since we've now shown that the existence of God precludes evil, it follows that the evil in the world requires the non-existence of God!

Analyzing the problem in this way is helpful, for it narrows down the kinds of reply we can give to it. Notice that not just *anything* we say (even if true) will be relevant as a reply. You must attack the argument. 'I don't like atheists!'

might be a truth about some Christians, and would be a truth in their autobiography, but it isn't a relevant reply to the argument, since it attacks neither the argument's content nor its structure. 'You're in need of God!' might be another truth (this one in the atheist's biography), but again, it's not a relevant reply. And since the structure of the argument seems to be good, our options are narrowed down even further. To get around the argument Christians are going to have to attack its *content*, and dispute one or more of the premises. And there are only three of those, so they don't have a lot of room for maneuver. *Which* premise should they attack?

Rejecting premise 3 — maybe God isn't perfect? Should they attack premise 3, which affirms that God is perfectly powerful and good? Should they say instead he *isn't* perfectly powerful and good? To state the question should be enough to answer it: of course not! Perhaps for some, whose view of reality is not informed by the Bible, that is a tempting way out of the problem of evil: define down God's attributes so that they 'fit' with the existence of evil. Just confess God as weak rather than perfectly powerful, or as somewhat malevolent rather than perfectly good. But for Christians who care about faithfulness to God's word, this is a non-starter, and would be a terrible witness to the skeptics they are trying to reach.

The Bible teaches that God is perfectly powerful. The Old Testament prophet Jeremiah confessed to God: 'Ah, Lord God! It is you who have made the heavens and the earth by your great power and by your outstretched arm! Nothing is too hard for you.' (Jer. 32:17). A few verses later God himself asks the rhetorical question: 'Behold, I am the Lord, the God of all flesh. Is anything too hard for me?' (Jer. 32:27). (The implied answer is supposed to be, 'Obviously not!') In the New Testament, when the angel Gabriel visits Mary the mother of Jesus, he says that 'nothing will be impossible with God' (Luke 1:37). And when Jesus was asked by his disciples whether anyone could be delivered from God's judgment on their own, apart from God's help, Jesus tells his disciples: 'With man this is impossible, but with God all things are possible' (Matt. 19:26). So, if Christians want to make a relevant reply to the problem of evil, they *have* to own up to the biblical teaching that God's power seems to be as perfect as power could possibly be.

Likewise for divine goodness. The apostle John repeatedly says that 'God is love' (1 John 4:8, 16). The Psalmist teaches us that 'The Lord is gracious and merciful, slow to anger and abounding in steadfast love. The Lord is good to all, and his mercy is over all that he has made…. The Lord is faithful in all his words and kind in all his works' (Ps. 145:8-9, 13). And after describing how God's goodness and generosity should lead us to be similarly generous and loving, Jesus sums up the point about God's goodness: 'You therefore must be perfect, as your heavenly Father is perfect' (Matt. 5:48).

Far better for Christians to say, 'I don't know how to get around your argument' than to say, 'I'm willing to reject the heart of the Christian confession about God in order to solve the problem of evil'! On a traditional understanding of God, and certainly on the view of God assumed for the purposes of this book, 'God' can be defined as the all-knowing, all-powerful, perfectly good creator and providential sustainer of the world. To the extent that the Bible indicates God is exactly this, to that extent Christians should be *unwilling* to reject premise 3. How strange for the Christian believer to say to the skeptic, 'Believe in the God of the Bible, despite evil! All you have to do is reject the God of the Bible!'

Rejecting premise 1 — maybe perfect power just can't prevent some evils? Perhaps then Christians should reject premise 1, and deny that 'a perfectly powerful being can prevent any evil.' Maybe bad things happen to good people because there are some evils that even a perfectly powerful God can't prevent. But why should we think this? God can prevent any case of moral evil by simply removing the free will by which it is done. Free will, however we define it, is after all a gift of God. And God can prevent any case of natural evil by suspending the natural processes that cause it. The laws of nature, whatever they are, are laws of a *nature* that is created by God and subject to God. So yes, 'a perfectly powerful being can prevent any evil.' There shouldn't be a doubt about this at all.

It's true that even a *perfectly* powerful God can't make square circles or married bachelors, because these tasks are contradictory, and so there's literally nothing (no thing) to be done. Likewise, it would be contradictory to 'prevent' two and two adding up to four, or to 'prevent' a universe created by God from being created by God. But there's nothing contradictory about intervening to prevent murder, rape, or theft. Ordinary human policemen aim to do this all the time, and they often succeed. And if this is possible on one occasion why not on all occasions? Can bad people or bad weather be more powerful than God? No, a perfectly powerful being can prevent any evil, and so premise 1 looks just as true as premise 3.

Rejecting premise 2 — maybe perfect goodness wouldn't prevent every evil? It seems Christians have one choice left: reject premise 2, which says that, 'A perfectly good being *will* prevent evil as far as he can.' But at first glance, doesn't this premise seem just as secure as the other two? If there were pain and suffering *you* could prevent, wouldn't you in your goodness seek to prevent it? Wouldn't you be a *bad* person for not preventing it? Well, maybe. But what if you had a *good reason* to permit the suffering? Would you still be bad?

Imagine an adult who inflicted pain on little children. Imagine he did this voluntarily (no one forces him to do it). Imagine that he gets *paid* for this activity, by the children's parents themselves! Indeed, imagine he does it *while the parents watch*. This seems like a perverse scenario, involving a moral monster if ever there was one. (Several moral monsters, in fact!) How could the adult possibly be regarded as good? But a moment's reflection can lead us to consider the possibilities. Maybe this adult is a dentist. Maybe the pain is an unfortunate but temporary by-product of a good thing he is bringing to pass: straightening children's teeth. And maybe the parents pay him, not because they *like* the pain, but because they trust the dentist, that he knows what he's doing and is making the best choices from start to finish. Here is a clear exception to premise 2, an exception which reveals that premise 2 is false. It is *not* the case that a good being would prevent evil (that is, significant cases of pain and suffering) as far as he can. The dentist can prevent all this pain and suffering—he can just quit his job. But his goodness doesn't require him to prevent it.

Likewise, imagine a parent who swoops down to swat away the hand of a toddler who is reaching out toward a live electrical outlet. The slap causes the toddler pain, perhaps enough to make it cry. The parent doesn't *have* to cause this pain; she can just walk on by, thereby preventing it. But she surely doesn't fail to be good because she didn't prevent pain she could prevent. Indeed, in this context, it seems good that she *does* inflict the pain!

These are merely analogies, of course, and pitifully inadequate ones at that, if their purpose is to bear the weight of the problem of evil. Their limitations are easy to see: dentists and parents have limited power, whereas God is almighty. But the point here isn't to solve the problem of evil in one go, but to see that premise 2 as it stands is false. It is not the case that a perfectly good being would prevent evil as far as he can. For *if you have a good reason that justifies you in permitting the pain*, then your goodness is not impugned.

The problem of evil comes down to this 'if.' '*If* God has a good reason….'

Either God has a reason that justifies him in permitting the evil in the world, or he does not. The problem of evil then, to be a good argument, must insist that God *doesn't* have such a reason. In the next chapter we will begin to explore this question, for 'theodicies' are justifications of the ways of God to men precisely because they spell out reasons God has for permitting the evil he does permit.

SUMMARY OF MAIN POINTS

- We must distinguish between merely asking questions about evil and proposing an argument against God from evil.
- Both the critic and the Christian bear a burden in this argument: the critic to spell out the argument and the Christian to reply to it.
- David Hume and Epicurus provide accessible statements of the problem of evil.
- Arguments are claims made in support of a concluding claim, and the problem of evil can certainly be stated as an argument.
- 'Evil' will be defined as 'any significant case of pain and suffering'.
- The 'you can't define evil' retort to the problem of evil fails to take the argument seriously. Indeed, it fails to engage with the argument at all!
- Both Christians and skeptics of Christianity recognize a distinction between moral evil and natural evil.
- Christians shouldn't get out of the problem by denying the perfection of God's attributes, or by affirming that God is weak.
- But one way to get out of the problem is to clarify that perfect goodness can permit evil as long as there are justifying reasons for permitting it. These reasons are

called 'theodicies,' which are stories that spell out the reasons God has for permitting the evil he does permit, and in this way attempt to justify the ways of God to men.

2

The Greater-Good Theodicy: A Threefold Argument for Three Biblical Themes

WHAT IS A THEODICY?

In the last chapter we distinguished questions from arguments. But we also saw that questions can be arguments in disguise. And if theodicies are an answer to the question, 'Why evil?' we must further distinguish the objective intellectual question '*Why* does God allow bad things?' from the personal existential question 'Why did God allow this bad thing to happen *to me*?' This book is primarily aimed at developing a solid answer to the first kind of question, and so I have narrowed the scope of this book accordingly. There is another volume in this series that attempts to answer the second, more personal kind of question. As a result, there is little in this volume that develops strategies for personally coping with pain and suffering on a daily basis (though I daresay some of the principles espoused in this book should at least *influence* such strategies!).

As noted in the Preface, the English word 'theodicy' comes from the two Greek words *theos* ('God') and *dike* ('justice' or 'justify'). So theodicies are attempts to justify God and his ways. We are familiar enough with this idea when it comes to justifying *ourselves*. When someone claims that *we* are in the wrong, that we are blameworthy for either doing something or for neglecting to do something, we are inclined to offer a justification of ourselves, defending ourselves from the charges by *offering reasons* why we are not blameworthy after all. (Of course, these reasons might differ depending on what the charges are.) Similarly, offering a theodicy—a justification of the ways of God to men— posits an exception to premise 2 of the problem of evil. The theodicy-minded Christian says, 'a perfectly good being *will* prevent evil as far as he can… *unless he has a good reason that justifies him in permitting that evil.*' If he *does* have a good reason, then it can't count against his goodness that he allows the evil.

Would just anything qualify as a theodicy? May Christians say any crazy thing on behalf of God and expect to be taken seriously? No, they should not. Typically, a theodicy has the following structure: there are goods that God is aiming at in his universe, but because of the kinds of goods God is aiming at, he cannot get them without permitting various evils. (Maybe this is because the evils must at least be *possible* if the goods are going to be possible. Or maybe this is because the evils must be *actual* if the goods are going to be actual. This question need not detain us now, though I will come back to it.)

In the Preface I said my theodicy was going to be that *the pain and suffering in God's world play a necessary role in bringing about greater goods that could not be brought about except for the presence of that pain and suffering. The world would be worse off without that pain and suffering, and so God is justified in pursuing the good by these means.* In stating the theodicy in this way—particularly, by using the words 'necessary role,' 'greater goods,' and 'worse off'—I recognized that there are at least two rules for theodicy, two assumptions behind all theodicies if they are to be genuine justifications of the ways of God to men. Let's look at these assumptions in turn.

Two assumptions behind all theodicy

The dependence of goods. The first assumption is about the 'dependence' of goods: the goods aimed at depend on and therefore require the evils. It has to be that God cannot get these various goods he is aiming at unless he permits the evils, for if he *could* get the goods without permitting the evils, then why wouldn't he do so? Wouldn't that be better?

(Of course!) But if, instead, the good is some sort of *response* to the evil—perhaps it is an overcoming of the evil, for instance—then clearly the good can't exist unless the evil does as well. For example, if it is a good thing for society to cooperate in order to defeat the threat of cancer, then there cannot be such cooperation unless there is the threat of cancer. Again, if it is a good thing to be brave in the face of battle, then there cannot be such bravery except in the face of battle (and so there must be battle). Later in this chapter, and more at length in chapter 4, we shall consider goods that have this kind of dependence on evils for their realization.

Given this dependence assumption, certain theodicies are immediately seen to be defective, and Christians should avoid them straightaway. What about fawns that suffer for days in the wake of a forest fire and then die? What goods could be connected to *that*? Well, I once had a student who said that such fawns 'had' to die so that future generations could get oil (the idea being that the fawn's corpse liquefies in the ground over ages and produces oil deposits for future oil-dependent humans). But this fails the dependence assumption, since clearly God could just *put* the oil in the ground, no fawns needed. In addition, even if there was some crazy law of the universe that required God to produce oil from fawn corpses, the real evil here is not the death of the fawn but the pain and suffering of the fawn. Why was *that* needed? Presumably God could have had the fawn die of a painless heart attack, and have still gotten the good of the oil, but without the evil of the suffering. This mini-theodicy offered by my well-meaning student simply doesn't work, because the goods aimed at (oil) could have been gotten *without* the attendant evils (pain and suffering of the fawn). In this case, the goods don't depend on the evils.

The weightiness of goods. The second assumption behind all theodicy is about the 'weightiness' of goods: the goods aimed at (by way of permitting the evils that make the goods possible) must be goods that are *worth pursuing*. Their goodness must be so great that they *outweigh* the evils they make possible or actual. Getting a pathetically *trivial* good by way of an enormous evil will have made the universe worse than it was before, since things would be better off with neither of those things than with them both. To illustrate, imagine if someone asserted that unless the Holocaust happened, the inventor of his favorite flavor of ice cream would not have existed (and he tells some crazy story that allegedly links the two things). *Even if* there is some dependence of the ice cream flavor on the Holocaust (extremely doubtful), this line of thinking can't possibly be a good theodicy, because the tradeoff wasn't worth it. Far better that the Holocaust *never* occurred, than that it occurs so we can get ice cream! The good here is just so trivial that no good person (not to mention a *perfectly* good person) would allow the Holocaust in order to aim at *that*! (Indeed, the sheer insensitivity of such an absurd theodicy *adds* to the sum total of evil in the world, rather than explaining it.)

So if the goods are not worth it, then no one is justified in pursuing them by these means. But what if I can overcome a bout of life-threatening cancer only if I submit to a painful but temporary regime of chemotherapy? Eradicating the cancer is a great good, and if I can overcome it through these temporary but painful means, then the tradeoff *is* worth it. 'Suffered chemotherapy, no more cancer' is a better situation than 'no chemotherapy, died of cancer.' In aiming to overcome the cancer by means of the chemotherapy, I am aiming at an outweighing good.

To summarize, the evils that are to be explained by way of theodicy will always be connected to *dependent* and *weighty* goods. Because they are dependent goods, evils *must* be permitted to get them. Because they are weighty goods, things are *better* with the goods (even with their attendant evils) than without the goods at all. So if every evil can be traced to a dependent, weighty good, then the task of theodicy has done its job.

THREE THEMES IN THE BIBLE THAT SUPPORT A GREATER-GOOD THEODICY

The Greater-Good theodicy says that the pain and suffering in God's world play a necessary role in bringing about greater goods that could not be brought about except for the presence of that pain and suffering. Is there anything *in the Bible* that encourages this point of view, at least in part? Christians believe that God has spoken in his written word (the Bible). Christians also believe that a fundamental theme of the Bible is God's response to evil. When responding to the problem of evil, therefore, Christians should not ignore any Bible passages which may shed light on God's relation to evil. These passages are there for a reason: to not only encourage the people of God, but to equip God's people to do every good work (2 Tim. 3:16-17), including the good work of defending God's goodness in the face of evil, by answering the questions of critics.

As the remainder of this chapter will show, three themes directly relevant to constructing a viable Greater-Good theodicy are repeatedly found in the Bible. Indeed, these three themes are quite often found *woven together in the same narrative*, in historical accounts that reveal the goodness of God in the midst of the world's evils. Again and again we see that (1) God aims at *great goods*, that (2) God often intends these great goods to come about *by way of various evils*, and that (3) God leaves created persons *in the dark* (in the dark about *which* goods are indeed his reasons for the evils, or about *how* the goods depend on the evils). That is, these narratives reveal *the goodness of God's purpose, the sovereignty of his providence* (including his sovereignty over evil), and *the inscrutability of his ways.* Such themes do not lie hidden in obscurity; they are right there on the surface of the biblical text. And Christians can incorporate them into an overall perspective on evil that is biblically faithful *and* that presents theodicy in a way that neutralizes the problem of evil. We turn now to three paradigm cases in the Bible, of God pursuing great goods by way of evils: Job, Joseph, and Jesus.

THE CASE OF JOB

The goodness of God's purpose. In the Old Testament book of Job, *God aims at a great good*: his own vindication. In particular, the vindication of his worthiness to be served for who he is rather than for the earthly goods he supplies. In the first chapter of the book, the 'prologue' before the main events, Satan challenged this in Job's case, insinuating instead that Job only served God because of what Job could get from God. Satan makes two predictions: 'But stretch out your hand and touch all that he has, and he will curse you to your face…. But stretch out your hand and touch his bone and his flesh, and he will curse you to your face'

(Job 1:11; 2:5). But God aims to refute Satan's charges, and frustrate Satan's predictions, by giving Job an opportunity to display great perseverance in the midst of great suffering. It is not possible, of course, to 'display great perseverance in the midst of great suffering,' without there being great suffering. And that is what we find.

The sovereignty of God's providence. In the book of Job, God intends the great good of the vindication of his own name to come to pass *by way of various evils* that come into Job's life. God uses five means to bring about this suffering. First, the Sabeans attacked, stealing Job's oxen and donkeys and striking down his servants (Job 1:15). Second, 'the fire of God fell from heaven and burned up the sheep and the servants and consumed them' (Job 1:16). Third, the Chaldeans attacked, stealing Job's camels and striking down more of his servants (Job 1:17). Fourth, 'a great wind came across the wilderness' and destroyed Job's house and family (Job 1:19). Fifth, Satan himself 'struck Job with loathsome sores from the sole of his foot to the crown of his head' (Job 2:7).

So what happened to Job was a combination of *moral evil* and *natural evil*, the moral evil being the Sabeans and Chaldeans stealing and murdering, and Satan inflicting ill health, and the natural evil being the fire and wind destroying buildings, animals, and people. But what is extraordinary is that *God* is the one who used these means to bring about the suffering! He was the one who was behind the suffering, the one who *ultimately* brought it to pass in Job's life. We know this because of three additional things that are said in the text.

First, after suffering the loss of his family, servants, and animals (but before the loss of his health), the Bible says:

> Then Job arose and tore his robe and shaved his head and fell on the ground and worshiped. And he said, 'Naked I came from my mother's womb, and naked shall I return. The LORD gave, and the LORD has taken away; blessed be the name of the LORD.' In all this Job did not sin or charge God with wrong (Job 1:21-22).

According to Job's own interpretation of the grievous events he has just suffered, who gave Job his family, servants, and animals? 'The LORD.' And who took it all away in a single day? 'The LORD.' This is not to deny that men and nature were clearly involved, for it is also true that *the Sabeans* took away, that *the Chaldeans* took away, that *the fire and wind* took away. But these were only instruments in the hands of God to bring to pass the purposes of God in Job's life. The Sabeans, Chaldeans, fire, and wind were the means by which *the LORD* took away. Job knew this. Job confessed this. The readers of the book are supposed to see this. Some might think that Job is going too far in attributing his sufferings to 'the LORD,' that he is sinning in some way by linking God too closely with his suffering. Perhaps his suffering itself is leading him to make this moral mistake! But the very next verse is clear: 'In all this Job did not sin or charge God with wrong' (Job 1:22). So in attributing his suffering to God, Job *wasn't* sinning and he *wasn't* charging God with wrongdoing. It was not sinful for Job to trace his suffering back to the will of God, and tracing it in this way was not to charge God with wrongdoing. The sovereignty of God's providence over evil seems to be an article of faith for Job. In his view, the Lord did it (v. 21), and the Lord was not wrong to do it (v. 22).

Second, after Job suffered his final indignity—the loss of his health at Satan's hands (Job 2:7)—his wife counseled him to give up his 'integrity,' to abandon his perseverance in remaining faithful to God. 'Curse God and die!' she says (Job 2:9). She reveals herself to be the kind of person that Satan was hoping Job would be, one who served God for what she could get from God, for the earthly goods that God supplies. But Job's rebuke to her reveals his continuing belief that God was the one behind his suffering:

> You speak as one of the foolish women would speak. Shall we receive good from God, and shall we not receive evil? (Job 2:10)

The ordinary Hebrew words for 'good' (*tōv*) and 'evil' (*rā'āh*) are used in this verse. Even as *tōv* is used to refer to a wide range of blessings in the Hebrew Bible, so *rā'āh* is used to refer to a wide range of suffering in the Hebrew Bible, including what we have defined as moral evil (Gen. 6:5; Jonah 1:2) and natural evil (Jonah 1:7; 4:6). According to this verse, in Job's view it would be foolishly inconsistent to think that only goods come from God and not evils as well. If God gives one, does he not have the right to give the other? Job seems to think so, and he was not sinning by tracing his suffering back to God in this way, for the verse continues: 'In all this Job did not sin with his lips' (Job 2:10).[1]

Third, Job's interpretation of his own suffering is confirmed to him by the rest of his family:

> Then came to him all his brothers and sisters and all who had known him before, and ate bread with him in his house. And they showed him sympathy and comforted him for all the evil that the LORD had brought upon him (Job 42:11).

They seemed to share Job's view of the matter: all of this evil (*rā'āh*) was something 'that the LORD had brought upon him.'

---

1 Later, when God specifically passes judgment on the various claims about him that have been spoken in the book, whereas Job's friends fare badly, Job's theology fares well. God says: 'My anger burns against you and against your two friends, for you have not spoken of me what is right, as my servant Job has' (Job 42:7).

The inscrutability of God's ways. In the book of Job, while God's providence is both good in its purpose and sovereign in its use of evils as means, it is obvious that God leaves Job completely *in the dark* about what God is doing. While we the readers have access to the story's prologue in chapter 1, and are therefore witnesses to Satan's charges against God and God's intention to refute those charges, Job himself is privy to none of this illuminating material. He doesn't know *which* goods God is aiming at by way of his sufferings, much less *how* such goods would depend on the evils he is suffering. Even at the end of the book, when God spends four chapters speaking to Job 'out of the whirlwind,' he never reveals to Job *why* he suffered. Instead, God describes Job as one who, by his accusations against God, 'darkens counsel by words without knowledge' (Job 38:2), exposing him as woefully ignorant of how God brought about the whole spectrum of created reality (Job 38:4–39:30; 40:6–41:34). In the midst of this extended divine interrogation Job hardly has time to catch his breath, daring only twice to offer a brief response, in order to confess his utter ignorance of God's ways:

> Then Job answered the LORD and said: 'Behold, I am of small account; what shall I answer you? I lay my hand on my mouth. I have spoken once, and I will not answer; twice, but I will proceed no further.' (Job 40:3-5)

> Then Job answered the LORD and said: 'I know that you can

do all things, and that no purpose of yours can be thwarted. "Who is this that hides counsel without knowledge?" Therefore I have uttered what I did not understand, things too wonderful for me, which I did not know. "Hear, and I will speak; I will question you, and you make it known to me." I had heard of you by the hearing of the ear, but now my eye sees you; therefore I despise myself, and repent in dust and ashes.' (Job 42:1–6)

Here Job confesses the absolute sovereignty of God ('I know that you can do all things, and that no purpose of yours can be thwarted') *and* the inscrutability of God's ways ('I have uttered what I did not understand, things too wonderful for me, which I did not know'). He accepts that God has made his case, that God is right to think that *Job* cannot put God in the wrong, that Job cannot condemn God so that Job may be in the right (Job 40:8–9). This is remarkable in light of Job's earlier complaint that by all appearances God makes no distinction between righteousness and wickedness (Job 9:21–24). On this basis he clearly desires an interview of some sort with God (Job 23:1–7). And in his last speech (chapters 26–31), Job claims that God has denied him justice (27:2), recounts the vivid contrast between how things once were (chapter 29) and how they now are (30:1–19), claims that God has been cruel and ruthless to him (30:20–23), gives a lengthy defense of his own life (31:1–34), and once again demands that God answer him and justify his ways to Job (31:35-37).

But at the end of the book, now that he has been confronted with his basic ignorance of how God brought about and sustains the physical world, Job realizes that he has little basis for concluding much of anything about whether God has good reasons for bringing about his suffering. Theologian John Frame summarizes God's rebuke: 'The point is that if Job is so ignorant concerning God's works in the natural world, how can he expect to understand the workings of God's mind in distributing good and evil?'[2] Job's friends are also condemned for their ignorance, for their presuming to have knowledge here. Their mistaken assumption was not that the Lord did it (in this both Job and his friends were correct), but that the Lord did it *to punish Job for his sins* (in this just about everyone in the book is dead wrong, not having access to the prologue that gives God's true reasons).

Thus in the book of Job, which is one of the most extended treatments of God's relation to evil in the entire Bible, we find the ingredients for a Greater-Good theodicy, for the idea that God brings about great goods by way of the evils on which those goods depend. But right alongside this we find reason for tempering any such theodicy with a large dose of divine inscrutability and therefore with creaturely humility. Job's inability to discern God's reason for his suffering was no argument that God didn't have a reason.

---

2   *Apologetics: A Justification of Christian Belief*, p. 175.

THE CASE OF JOSEPH

The goodness of God's purpose. In the Old Testament narrative about Joseph (who was one of the twelve sons of Jacob, and therefore an ancestor of later Israelites), *God aims at great goods*: saving the broader Mediterranean world from a famine, preserving his people in the midst of such danger, and fulfilling openly his promise to preserve his people. This is not only so they can survive to be a great nation in the land of Canaan, but that they might ultimately bring into the world the Savior of the world, for Jesus was an Israelite descended from the Israelites who existed in Joseph's day (Matt. 1:1–17 and Luke 3:23–38). That is, the good which God aimed at was nothing less than redemption for any and all who would place their faith in this Savior who would come.

The narrative about Joseph occurs in the first book of the Bible, specifically in Genesis 37–50. This book forms a crucial prologue to the next four books (Exodus, Leviticus, Numbers, and Deuteronomy), for it recounts the historical journey God's people took from the day Abraham their forefather was called out of Chaldea (Gen. 12) to the time they were settled in the land of Egypt (Gen. 47). This journey set the stage for God's eventual deliverance of Abraham's descendants from slavery in Egypt (Exod. 12–14), his making them his people by way of covenant (Exod. 24), and his bringing them into the land of Canaan by way of judgment on the land's previous inhabitants, in order to continue his covenant relationship with the Israelites (Josh. 1–24) until Jesus entered the world.

By the time we get to Joseph's story in Genesis, God's redemptive purposes will shortly be 'hanging by a thread,' historically speaking, for a famine will eventually arise in both Egypt and Canaan that threatens the livelihood of Abraham's descendants (Gen. 47:13). Prior to the famine, in order that his people may be spared starvation and thereby continue to help realize God's redemptive purposes for the world, God raises up Joseph to be Pharaoh king of Egypt's 'right-hand man' (Gen. 41:37–45). In this capacity Joseph will be one who administers a wise plan that enables the sufficient distribution of food in time of need (Gen. 41:46–49; 41:53–57; 47:13–26), and who is the means of the Israelites resettling in Egypt under Pharaoh's protection (Gen. 46:1–27; 47:1–12; 47:27).

The sovereignty of God's providence. In the Old Testament narrative about Joseph, it is also evident that God intends this great good of the preservation of his people to come to pass *by way of various evils*. The story has many twists and turns: stirred up by jealousy, Joseph's brothers first conspire to kill him (Gen. 37:18–20), then leave him for dead in the bottom of a pit (Gen. 37:21–24), then sell him into slavery to Midianite traders who take (the now captive) Joseph into Egypt (Gen. 37:25–28). The moral evil suffered by Joseph continues. He is sold by the slavers to Potiphar (an officer of Pharaoh, king of Egypt; Gen. 39:1), falsely accused by Potiphar's wife of attempted rape (Gen. 39:7–18), thrown into Pharaoh's prison on the basis of this false charge (Gen. 39:19–20), and has his plight completely forgotten by Pharaoh's cupbearer, one who had promised to Joseph that he would bring his case to Pharaoh (Gen. 40:14–15; 40:23).

Joseph's skills at interpreting dreams are eventually remembered by Pharaoh's cupbearer (Gen. 41:9–13), and this is the means of Joseph finally being released from prison, serving as the interpreter of Pharaoh's dreams, and in reward being promoted as Pharaoh's assistant (Gen. 41:14–46). After Joseph resettles his and his father's family to Egypt in the time of famine, his father Jacob dies, and it is at this point that fear grips the hearts of Joseph's brothers. They are terrified that Joseph will now enact some sort of revenge upon them for the 'evil' (*rā'āh*) they inflicted on Joseph so many years prior (Gen. 50:15–18). There is no more father Jacob to displease if Joseph decides to deal out brutal retribution to his brothers for their betrayal! And yet at the precise moment when one would expect Joseph to seek vengeance, we find him both comforting and instructing his brothers with the sovereign providence of God in the midst of their evil:

But Joseph said to them, 'Do not fear, for am I in the place of God? As for you, you meant evil (*rā'āh*) against me, but God meant it for good (*tōv*), to bring it about that many people should be kept alive, as they are today. So do not fear; I will provide for you and your little ones.' Thus he comforted them and spoke kindly to them. (Gen. 50:19–21)

Having so expertly interpreted Pharaoh's dreams about the forthcoming famine, Joseph applies these same interpretive skills to the 'dream' of his own past life. On Joseph's understanding, *we have one set of events*: the betrayal of Joseph by his brothers, his being left for dead, his being sold into slavery. Given our definitions in chapter 1 these are *moral evils*, bringing about the social and psychological suffering that attended Joseph's involuntary separation from his own family (including separation from his own parents), and ensuring the physical suffering of Joseph's numerous 'lost years' in Pharaoh's dungeons. Both Joseph's brothers (Gen. 50:15, 17) and Joseph himself (Gen. 50:20) see what Joseph has suffered as genuine 'evil' done to him by responsible human beings. But while we have one set of events, according to Genesis 50:20 *we have two sets of intentions with respect to those events*. Joseph's brothers 'meant evil.' That was their intent, their goal. But *God* meant it with another intention or purpose in mind: great 'good' (*tōv*), 'to bring it about that many people should be kept alive, as they are today.'

So Joseph's brothers and God are intending the *same* set of events: the moral evil that Joseph suffered. But although God meant the evil events which befell Joseph, he meant them *for good*, and it's the divine intention behind these events that makes all the difference in the world. Joseph seems quite willing to praise God for God's good intentions with respect to the events which befell Joseph, even while Joseph recognized the sin of his brothers because of *their* intentions with respect to those same events. They are blamed for their intending of the act for evil, while God is praised by Joseph for his intending of the act for a greater good, as he providentially took it up into his all-wise plan. As in the case of Job's sufferings, so here with Joseph's sufferings: God meant the evil done by the perpetrators (that it would in fact take place), but he meant it for good.

Earlier, Joseph told his brothers to 'not be distressed or angry with yourselves because you sold me here, for *God sent me* before you to preserve life… And *God sent me* before you to preserve for you a remnant on earth, and to keep alive for you many survivors' (Gen. 45:5, 7; my emphasis). So on Joseph's view it was ultimately *God* who sent him into Egypt, and this view is confirmed by Psalm 105, a psalm devoted to retelling God's 'wondrous works': 'When he summoned a famine on the land and broke all supply of bread, he had sent a man ahead of them, Joseph, who was sold as a slave' (vv. 16–17). Who was it who 'sent a man ahead of them,

Joseph,' to be 'sold as a slave'? One would think that it was Joseph's brothers (who sold Joseph into slavery), or the Midianite traders (who received him into slavery). These answers would not be false ones. But ultimately it was God who sent Joseph into Egypt. The betrayal and being sold into slavery was the *means* of that divine sending—it is *how* God sent him. Indeed, quite mysteriously, God is the one who 'summoned a famine on the land and broke all supply of bread' (Ps. 105:16; cf. Gen. 41:32). So God seems to have intended both the moral evil (the betrayal) and the natural evil (the famine) that occurred in the Genesis narrative. He intended that the great good of the preservation of his people, and the fulfillment of his promise to preserve them, would come to pass by way of these various evils.

The inscrutability of God's ways. In the Old Testament narrative about Joseph, God leaves various human beings *in the dark* that great goods are indeed his reason for the evils, or even that *there is* a reason for the evils. It is true that in some way Joseph ultimately gains knowledge that God intended the events for good. (Or was this just part of his overall view of God, without God having to explicitly reveal it to him?) And as we have seen, Joseph in turn shares this encouraging perspective with his brothers at the very end of the book. But *when these evils were committed*, neither Joseph's brothers, nor the Midianite traders, nor Potiphar's wife, nor the cupbearer, knew the role their blameworthy actions would play in preserving God's people in a time of danger. No one at the time would have had a clue as to *which* goods depended on which evils, or that the evils would even work towards *any* goods at all! As in the case of Job, so here in the case of Joseph, we again find the ingredients for a Greater-Good theodicy tempered by divine inscrutability. Unerring, specific divine purposes for specific greater goods are thereby hidden from us. We would have no basis (apart from God's revealing this) to conclude he even *has* these purposes in these situations. But it also follows from our ignorance that we would have no basis to *rule out* his having such purposes either. Developing this point into a credible role that the Greater-Good theodicy can play in a viable response to the intellectual problem of evil is a task for chapter 4.

THE CASE OF JESUS

The goodness of God's purpose. In the Bible, *God aims at a great good*: the redemption of his people by the atonement of Christ. The death of Christ on the cross is repeatedly set forth in the Bible as that which turns aside the wrath of God for all who trust in him. Jesus lived the perfect life we ought to have lived, and died the death for sin that we ought to die for our own sins. Based on this perfect atonement for sin,

God freely forgives the sins of all who trust in Jesus. Because Jesus is divine, Jesus's sacrifice has infinite value before God. Because Jesus is human, Jesus's sacrifice is appropriately on behalf of his fellow humans, who owe God a life of perfect obedience and who are liable to God's just judgment because of their sin. The cross is God's perfect solution to our worst problem imaginable, and so one might think that God's aiming at this good is his aiming at the highest imaginable good we could receive!

In addition, the cross glorifies God and exalts him in all of his attributes. In it we see displayed the justice of God (who judges our sin in Jesus), the love, grace, and mercy of God (who provides the very atonement we need, even though we are sinners and do not deserve to be saved from our sin), the wisdom of God (who devised this plan of redemption that is perfectly suited to our need), and the power of God (who revealed this plan little by little as Bible history progressed over the span of at least 4,000 years, and who orchestrated history so that events happened precisely as predicted). Apart from the cross, we creatures would never have an opportunity to know, love, and worship God in these respects. Whole aspects of God's character would be unrevealed to us. So the cross may secure the highest imaginable good *for God* as well—his being glorified for all of eternity for being who he *really* is, the God of salvation. In aiming at the cross, then, God may have been aiming at the greatest good for *both* God and man, that is, the greatest good imaginable!

The sovereignty of God's providence. In the Bible, God intends this great good to come to pass *by way of various evils*: the plots against Jesus by the Jewish leaders at the time (Matt. 26:3–4, 14-15), Satan's prompting of Judas that he should betray Jesus (John 13:21–30), Judas's actual betrayal of Jesus (Matt. 26:47–56; 27:3–10), the obviously unjust 'show trials' that wrongly convicted Jesus of blasphemy (Matt. 26:57–68), Pilate's cowardice in condemning a clearly innocent man to brutal death (Matt. 27:15–26), and the Roman soldiers' carrying out of this sentence (Matt. 27:27–44). This perplexing chain of perverse moral evil stretches from the inauguration of Jesus's public teaching ministry until his dying moments on the cross, and the removal of any link in this chain would have robbed the world of Jesus's crucifixion, and therefore of the highest good for both man and God.

In the wake of what Jesus accomplished for the world through his death, burial, and resurrection from the dead, the early church preached the good news (i.e., 'gospel') of this divine accomplishment for human beings, summoning their hearers to repentance from their sins and to faith in this exalted Savior. Such preaching in turn provoked heated responses from the Jewish leaders of the day, many of whom (but not all!) rejected this gospel message, and sought to prevent its preaching, by force if necessary. On one such occasion, the Jewish leaders confronted Peter and John (two of Jesus's representatives, or 'apostles'), arrested them for preaching Jesus, put them into custody and then finally released them. At that point, Peter and John's friends prayed that the same God who sovereignly put Jesus on the cross would sovereignly protect them from persecution and give them boldness in preaching this same Jesus. Here is their prayer, which affords us a crucial insight into how early Christians viewed Jesus's sufferings:

> 'Why did the Gentiles rage, and the peoples plot in vain? The kings of the earth set themselves, and the rulers were gathered together, against the LORD and against his Anointed'—for truly in this city there were gathered together against your holy servant Jesus, whom you anointed, both Herod and Pontius Pilate, along with the Gentiles and the peoples of Israel, to do whatever your hand and your plan had predestined to take place. And now, LORD, look upon their threats and grant to your servants to continue to speak your word with all boldness…. (Acts 4:25–29)

The early Christian believers' view of the sufferings of Jesus was like Job's view of his sufferings, and Joseph's view of his sufferings. Apparently, taking such a view was a natural and consistent pattern among the people of God throughout biblical history. In this case, the early Christians believed God planned that the responsible human beings who perpetrated these moral evils would in fact do so. Specific people—not only 'Gentiles' and 'peoples of Israel' but 'Herod' and 'Pontius Pilate'—were 'gathered together… to do whatever your hand and your plan had predestined to take place.' 'Whatever' these people did against Jesus, two things are true: it was determined in advance ('predestined') by God himself, and yet these individuals are guilty before God for doing that which was determined in advance. Therefore, earlier in the prayer, it is said that the people 'plot in vain.' What they plot against Jesus is surely sinful, but it is a *vain* plot—futile and useless—because (unbeknown to them) whatever these hostile individuals intended was simply the fulfillment of God's prior plan. *They* intend it for evil, but *God* intends it for good, to the (spiritual) saving of many lives.

Surely the murder of the innocent Jesus was a wicked act. And yet God planned that this evil would take place to bring about a greater good (Acts 3:18). Indeed, God revealed this plan centuries earlier, and this plan included the innocent Jesus being oppressed and afflicted unto death (Isa. 53), Judas's betrayal of Jesus (Acts 1:15–20; John 13:18; 17:12; cf. Ps. 41:9; 109:8), and even the soldiers dividing Jesus's garments (John 19:23–24; cf. Ps. 22:18). In explaining that Jesus was indeed the fulfillment of divine prophecy and plan, the apostle Peter (another 'apostle' or chosen representative of Jesus) preached that 'this Jesus, delivered up according to the definite plan and foreknowledge of God, you crucified and killed by the hands of lawless men' (Acts 2:23). Peter says that Jesus was not just delivered by the foreknowledge of God, but by the 'definite plan' of God. And yet the very hands which carry out the specific divine intentions with respect to Jesus are 'lawless' hands, and thus subject to God's judgment (Luke 22:22). Once again there is *one set of events*, but *two sets of intentions* behind the events: human and divine. The human intentions were evil, and therefore brought about an evil act. The divine intentions were good, because the goal was to bring about a greater good.

The inscrutability of God's ways. In the Bible, God leaves various human agents *in the dark* that this greater good is indeed his reason for the evils: the Jewish leaders, Satan, Judas, Pilate, and the soldiers are all ignorant of the role they play in fulfilling the divinely prophesied redemptive purpose by the cross of Christ. They had *other* purposes in mind: the Jewish leaders intended to end Jesus's alleged blasphemy of claiming to be equal to God, Satan intended that Jesus's ministry would be an utter failure, Judas intended to earn his silver, Pilate intended to quell growing Jewish discontent before it reached unmanageable proportions, and the soldiers intended to earn their pay. The apostle Paul preached on this theme in a first-century Jewish synagogue, claiming that:

> those who live in Jerusalem and their rulers, because they
> did not recognize him nor understand the utterances of the
> prophets, which are read every Sabbath, fulfilled them by
> condemning him. And though they found in him no guilt
> worthy of death, they asked Pilate to have him executed.
> And when they had carried out all that was written of him,
> they took him down from the tree and laid him in a tomb.
> (Acts 13:27–29)

They were ignorant 'because they did not recognize him.'
They were ignorant because they did not 'understand the
utterances of the prophets.' And yet in their ignorance they
'fulfilled them by condemning him'—that is, fulfilled the
prophets by condemning Jesus—and thus unknowingly
'carried out all that was written of him.' And unless *we* had
a divinely revealed written commentary on this extremely
important stretch of history—that is, unless we had the
Gospels, the Acts of the Apostles, and the Letters of the
New Testament—we wouldn't know any of this either! We
would be just as ignorant of these greater goods as those who
perpetrated these evils.

In introducing these three points about 'the case of
Jesus'—about the goodness of God's purpose, the sovereignty
of God's providence, and the inscrutability of God's
ways—I have repeatedly said these are points found 'in the

Bible', rather than merely 'in this book' or 'in this narrative.' That's because the message of the cross truly spans the entire Bible, Old Testament and New Testament. As my citations illustrate, it is impossible to restrict that message to a certain book or passage in the Bible. One might think, therefore, that the cross of Jesus is quite central to God's dealings with the world, and offers us an especially valuable insight as to God's *modus operandi* (his 'way of working') when it comes to pursuing great goods for his creation. The Job and Joseph narratives are significant but limited anticipations of the grand revelation in Jesus that God wisely and powerfully takes the worst evils and works them out for the greatest goods, in ways unanticipated by any humans on the scene. The Greater-Good theodicy, to the extent that one can be constructed from these materials, would seem to reflect profound and pervasive truths to which all Christians are already committed. Christians therefore should be wary of pushing these truths to the periphery in their reflections on the problem of evil, much less of departing from the Bible's point of view, even temporarily, to defend the Bible's point of view.

The *message* of the cross reveals to us the marvelous, unexpected way in which God confronts and overcomes the evil of our hearts: by sending the one who lived the life we ought to have lived, and who died the death we ought to have died. But the *method* of the cross reveals to us that

God's overcoming the evil of our hearts rests upon God's using the evils of the world to get the cross (because he uses the evil decisions of Satan, Judas, the Jewish leaders, Pilate, and the Roman soldiers, all of which resulted in the suffering of the cross). The message and method of the cross is in effect God's double victory over evil, and a double revelation of the powerful love of God in the midst of evil.

CONCLUSION

Questions raised. In writing (and reading) a book on the problem of evil, it sometimes seems that attempted answers simply raise more questions! I have deliberately restricted the scope of this chapter to considering the two assumptions behind theodicy in general—they involve God's aiming at weighty, dependent goods—and to considering three biblically-derived themes in support of the Greater-Good theodicy in particular—great goods, evils as means to the goods, and human ignorance of the goods and how they depend on the evils. But my presentation so far will no doubt raise certain questions in the minds of thoughtful readers.

First, the Greater-Good theodicy seems to bring God into far too close of a relation to evil. Regardless of what these three 'cases' have allegedly shown us, is it really true that God ordains evils so that good may come? Doesn't the Bible expressly forbid this (Rom. 3:8)? And are we really to think that this could be God's relation to *all* of the evils in the world? Job, Joseph, and Jesus seem a paltry foundation for such a sweeping view.

Second, at least some of the Greater-Good theodicy presented in these biblical passages doesn't seem to satisfy the very definition of theodicy that was earlier endorsed! Just as God could get the oil to future generations without the pain and suffering of the fawn, couldn't God have preserved the Israelites *without* Joseph playing his painful role at all? (Why not just appoint a Pharaoh who would mercifully distribute food to the Israelites? Why not just dispense with the famine altogether?) Did God *have* to vindicate his name in response to Satan's charges? Why not tell Satan to take a hike, and spare Job all the suffering? It surely seems that in some of these cases, either God should have declined to aim at the goods he did aim at (the goods weren't weighty enough), or he could have gotten the goods without the evils (the goods weren't dependent enough).

Licensing and limiting the Greater-Good theodicy. In response to these concerns, I will try to *license* and *limit* the Greater-Good theodicy in the next two chapters. First, in the next chapter, I will argue that the relation God sustains to evil in the Job, Joseph, and Jesus passages is not an anomaly, but part and parcel of a more general view the Bible takes on the subject, with respect to both natural and moral evil. He is sovereign over it all. In addition, making and defending a relevant distinction between doing evil and ordaining evil will help to ward off the idea that God is somehow blameworthy for intending these evils for good. These points will go a long way toward licensing the Greater-Good theodicy as something Christians can and ought to use in response to the problem of evil.

Second, in chapter 4 I will further develop the theme of divine inscrutability by way of the Bible, and defend it philosophically. Yes, it seems to us that in many cases God can get these goods without the evils, but is that really true? If instead we are 'in the dark' about these dependencies, then this ignorance on our part will not only limit the kinds of ways that Christians should apply the Greater-Good theodicy in the face of suffering; it will also limit the ways the Greater-Good theodicy can be objected to as a viable solution to the problem of evil.

SUMMARY OF MAIN POINTS

- A 'theodicy' gives a reason God could have for permitting evil, a reason that justifies God in permitting the evil, and that is consistent with God's attributes of perfect power and goodness.

- The 'Greater-Good theodicy' says that the pain and suffering in God's world play a necessary role in bringing about greater goods that could not be brought about except for the presence of that pain and suffering. Since the world would be worse off without that pain and suffering, God is justified in pursuing the good by these means.

- There are two assumptions behind all theodicy: the dependence of the goods and the weightiness of the goods. That is, the goods God is aiming at must depend on and therefore require the evils, and the goods aimed at must be so great that they outweigh the evils.

- There are three themes in the Bible that support a Greater-Good theodicy: the goodness of God's purpose, the sovereignty of God's providence, and the inscrutability of God's ways. We see these three themes brought together when the Bible describes the sufferings of Job, Joseph, and Jesus.

- In order to respond to two key objections to this approach, the Greater-Good theodicy will be both 'licensed' and 'limited' in the next two chapters.

3

Licensing the Greater-Good Theodicy: God's Sovereignty over Evil

INTRODUCTION

In chapter 2, after clarifying the nature of theodicy, we sought a biblical basis for the Greater-Good theodicy, for the view that the pain and suffering in God's world play a necessary role in bringing about greater goods that could not be brought about except for the presence of that pain and suffering. I claimed that we find a basis for this theodicy, at least in part, in the cases of Job, Joseph, and Jesus. (We find it in several other biblical passages as well; see the Appendix at the end of this book.) But questions raised at the end of that chapter indicated that we are not yet licensed to use this theodicy as a *general* response to the problem of evil. Two of those questions will be addressed in this chapter, as we further examine the Bible.[1]

---

1   The third question raised will be addressed in the next chapter.

First, are we really to think that God is the one who ultimately decides whether *any* evil comes to pass in his world, and then *ensures* that the evil comes to pass? Such a sweeping view seems to go far beyond what we find in the Job, Joseph, and Jesus passages, and yet such a sweeping view seems needed if the Greater-Good theodicy is to provide a solution to the problem of evil (and not just to isolated instances of evil).

Second, even if God exercises this kind of sovereignty over evil, doesn't this just make the problem of evil *worse*? How can we bring God into such close relation to evil, without God himself becoming evil? Doesn't God forbid that we do evil so that good may come (Rom. 3:8)? What becomes of this moral principle in the context of the Greater-Good theodicy? In chapter 1 we found reason to affirm premise 3 of the problem of evil: 'God is perfectly powerful and good.' But this 'solution' to the problem seems to deny this, making God himself to be evil rather than good.

In the remainder of this chapter, I'll answer the first question by considering numerous biblical passages that considerably widen the scope of God's sovereignty over natural and moral evil. What we learned in the last chapter is not an exception to but several instances of a broader teaching about God spread liberally through the Bible. I'll then answer the second question by drawing and defending a distinction that not only preserves but *argues for* God's moral innocence in the midst of his sovereignly intending evils for good. Finally, I'll draw out some implications of these points for both Christians and critics who dialogue about the problem of evil.

GOD'S SOVEREIGNTY OVER NATURAL EVIL

In chapter 1 natural evil was defined as significant pain and suffering in the world that is *not* caused by free persons either intentionally or through culpable neglect of their responsibilities. Natural evil comes from 'how nature goes on,' being caused by impersonal objects and forces quite independently of human choices. These include famine, drought, rampaging wild animals, disease, birth defects such as blindness and deafness, and even death itself. But the Bible presents multitudes of examples of God intentionally bringing about each of these things (rather than being someone who merely permits nature to 'do its thing' on its own). In addition to the fire, wind, and disease visited upon Job, his family, and his livestock, here is just a selection of further examples of the 'divine intentionality' view of these natural evils (italics added for emphasis):

Famine

> And *I will heap disasters upon them*; I will spend my arrows on them; *they shall be wasted with hunger*, and devoured by plague and poisonous pestilence; I will send the teeth of

beasts against them, with the venom of things that crawl in the dust. (Deut. 32:23–24)

Now Elisha had said to the woman whose son he had restored to life, 'Arise, and depart with your household, and sojourn wherever you can, for *the Lord has called for a famine*, and it will come upon the land for seven years.' (2 Kings 8:1)

When *he summoned a famine on the land and broke all supply of bread*…. (Ps. 105:16)

For behold, *the Lord God of hosts is taking away* from Jerusalem and from Judah support and supply, *all support of bread*, and all support of water…. (Isa. 3:1)

Moreover, he said to me, 'Son of man, behold, *I will break the supply of bread in Jerusalem.* They shall eat bread by weight and with anxiety, and they shall drink water by measure and in dismay.' (Ezek. 4:16)

…when I send against you the deadly arrows of famine, arrows for destruction, which I will send to destroy you, and *when I bring more and more famine upon you and break your supply of bread.* (Ezek. 5:16)

I will send famine and wild beasts against you, and they will rob you of your children. Pestilence and blood shall pass through you, and I will bring the sword upon you. I am the Lord; I have spoken. (Ezek. 5:17)

Son of man, when a land sins against me by acting faithlessly, and *I stretch out my hand against it and break its supply of bread and send famine upon it*, and cut off from it man and beast…. (Ezek. 14:13)

For thus says the Lord God: How much more *when I send upon Jerusalem* my four disastrous acts of judgment, sword, *famine*, wild beasts, and pestilence, to cut off from it man and beast! (Ezek. 14:21)

Therefore I will take back my grain in its time, and my wine in its season, and I will take away my wool and my flax, which were to cover her nakedness. (Hosea 2:9)

'*I gave you cleanness of teeth in all your cities, and lack of bread in all your places*, yet you did not return to me,' declares the Lord… '*I struck you with blight and mildew*; your many gardens and your vineyards, your fig trees and your olive trees *the locust devoured*; yet you did not return to me,' declares the Lord. (Amos 4:6, 9)

I struck you and all the products of your toil with blight and with mildew and with hail, yet you did not turn to me, declares the Lord. (Hag. 2:17)

Drought

The Lord will strike you with wasting disease and with fever, inflammation and fiery heat, and with *drought* and with blight and with mildew. They shall pursue you until you perish. (Deut. 28:22)

When heaven is shut up and *there is no rain because they have sinned against you*, if they pray toward this place and acknowledge your name and turn from their sin, when you afflict them…. (1 Kings 8:35)

For behold, *the* Lord *God of hosts is taking away* from Jerusalem and from Judah support and supply, all support of bread, and *all support of water*…. (Isa. 3:1)

…lest I strip her naked and make her as in the day she was born, and make her like a wilderness, *and make her like a parched land, and kill her with thirst.* (Hosea 2:3)

'I gave you cleanness of teeth in all your cities, and lack of bread in all your places, yet you did not return to me,' declares the Lord. '*I also withheld the rain from you* when there were yet three months to the harvest; *I would send rain on one city, and send no rain on another city*; one field would have rain, and *the field on which it did not rain would wither*; so two or three cities would wander to another city to drink water, *and would not be satisfied*; yet you did not return to me,' declares the Lord. (Amos 4:6–8)

And *I have called for a drought on the land and the hills*, on the grain, the new wine, the oil, on what the ground brings forth, on man and beast, and on all their labors. (Hag. 1:11)

Rampaging wild animals

And *I will let loose the wild beasts against you*, which shall bereave you of your children and destroy your livestock and make you few in number, so that your roads shall be deserted. (Lev. 26:22)

Then the LORD sent fiery serpents among the people, and they bit the people, so that many people of Israel died. (Num. 21:6)

And I will heap disasters upon them; I will spend my arrows on them; they shall be wasted with hunger, and devoured by plague and poisonous pestilence; *I will send the teeth of beasts against them*, with the venom of things that crawl in the dust. (Deut. 32:23–24)

And at the beginning of their dwelling there, they did not fear the LORD. Therefore *the LORD sent lions among them, which killed some of them.* (2 Kings 17:25)

'For behold, *I am sending among you serpents, adders that cannot be charmed, and they shall bite you*,' declares the LORD. (Jer. 8:17)

I will send famine and *wild beasts against you*, and they will rob you of your children. Pestilence and blood shall pass through you, and I will bring the sword upon you. I am the LORD; I have spoken. (Ezek. 5:17)

If I cause wild beasts to pass through the land, and they ravage it, and it be made desolate, so that no one may pass through because of the beasts…. (Ezek. 14:15)

For thus says the Lᴏʀᴅ God: How much more *when I send upon Jerusalem* my four disastrous acts of judgment, sword, famine, *wild beasts*, and pestilence, to cut off from it man and beast! (Ezek. 14:21)

Say this to them, Thus says the Lᴏʀᴅ God: As I live, surely those who are in the waste places shall fall by the sword, and *whoever is in the open field I will give to the beasts to be devoured*, and those who are in strongholds and in caves shall die by pestilence. (Ezek. 33:27)

Disease

…then I will do this to you: *I will visit you* with panic, *with wasting disease and fever* that consume the eyes and make the heart ache. And you shall sow your seed in vain, for your enemies shall eat it. (Lev. 26:16)

And I will bring a sword upon you, that shall execute vengeance for the covenant. And if you gather within your cities, *I will send pestilence among you*, and you shall be delivered into the hand of the enemy. (Lev. 26:25)

I will strike them with the pestilence and disinherit them, and I will make of you a nation greater and mightier than they. (Num. 14:12)

The Lord *will make the pestilence stick to you* until he has consumed you off the land that you are entering to take possession of it. (Deut. 28:21)

The Lord *will strike you with wasting disease* and with fever, inflammation and fiery heat, and with drought and with blight and with mildew. They shall pursue you until you perish. (Deut. 28:22)

The Lord *will strike you with the boils of Egypt, and with tumors and scabs and itch*, of which you cannot be healed. (Deut. 28:27)

And the Lord *touched the king, so that he was a leper to the day of his death*, and he lived in a separate house. And Jotham the king's son was over the household, governing the people of the land. (2 Kings 15:5; cf. 2 Chron. 26:19-20)

…behold, *the* Lord *will bring a great plague* on your people, your children, your wives, and all your possessions. (2 Chron. 21:14)

Birth defects such as blindness and deafness

Then the Lord said to him, 'Who has made man's mouth? Who makes him mute, or deaf, or seeing, or blind? *Is it not I, the* Lord*?*' (Exod. 4:11)

As he passed by, he saw a man blind from birth. And his disciples asked him, 'Rabbi, who sinned, this man or his parents, that he was born blind?' Jesus answered, 'It was not that this man sinned, or his parents, *but that the works of God might be displayed in him.*' (John 9:1–3)[2]

Death itself

See now that I, even I, am he, and there is no god beside me; *I kill and I make alive; I wound and I heal*; and there is none that can deliver out of my hand. (Deut. 32:39)

The LORD kills and brings to life; he brings down to Sheol and raises up. The LORD makes poor and makes rich; he brings low and he exalts. (1 Sam. 2:6–7)

Ten Egyptian plagues. Turning the Nile river to blood (Exod. 7:14–24), swarms of frogs from the Nile river (8:1–15), swarms of gnats (8:16–19), swarms of flies (8:20–32), death of Egyptian livestock (9:1–7), boils on the skin of men and animals (9:8–12), hailstones (9:13–35), swarms of locusts (10:1–20), total darkness (10:21–29), death of firstborn Egyptians (11:4–10; 12:12–13, 27–30).

'Impersonal' forces and objects. With respect to these and many other kinds of natural disaster (tornados, hurricanes,

---

2   A divine purpose or intent is implied behind this man's blindness from birth. It is not ultimately a 'random', purposeless mutation which brought this about, but the divine purpose.

tsunami, avalanches, forest fires, earthquakes), we typically trace these to the impersonal objects and forces that bring them about (wind, water, clouds, snow, lightning, fire, earth). But the Bible presents these objects and forces as proximate causes at best, being always under the *ultimate* control of God and *always* doing his bidding.

> *You visit the earth and water it*; you greatly enrich it; *the river of God* is full of water; you provide their grain, for so you have prepared it. *You water its furrows* abundantly, settling its ridges, *softening it with showers*, and blessing its growth. You crown the year with your bounty; your wagon tracks overflow with abundance. (Ps. 65:9–11)

> The crash of *your thunder* was in the whirlwind; *your lightnings* lighted up the world; the earth trembled and shook. (Ps. 77:18)

> O my God, make them like whirling dust, like chaff before the wind. As fire consumes the forest, as the flame sets the mountains ablaze, so may you pursue them with *your tempest* and terrify them with *your hurricane*! (Ps. 83:13–15)

> *His lightnings* light up the world; the earth sees and trembles. (Ps. 97:4)

He makes his messengers *winds*, his ministers a *flaming fire*. (Ps. 104:4; cf. 104:10–24)

For he commanded and raised *the stormy wind*, which lifted up *the waves of the sea*…. He made *the storm* be still, and *the waves of the sea* were hushed. (Ps. 107:25, 29)

Whatever the Lord pleases, he does, in heaven and on earth, in the *seas* and all deeps. He it is who makes the *clouds* rise at the end of the earth, who makes *lightnings* for the rain and brings forth the *wind* from his storehouses. (Ps. 135:6–7)

He covers the heavens with *clouds*; he prepares *rain* for the earth; he makes grass grow on the hills. (Ps. 147:8)

He gives *snow* like wool; he scatters *frost* like ashes. He hurls down his *crystals of ice* like crumbs; who can stand before his *cold*? He sends out his word, and melts them; he makes his *wind* blow and the *waters* flow. (Ps. 147:16–18)

Praise the Lord from the earth, you great sea creatures and all deeps, *fire and hail, snow and mist, stormy wind fulfilling his word!* (Ps. 148:7–8)

But *the Lord hurled a great wind upon the sea*, and there was a mighty tempest on the sea, so that the ship threatened to break up. (Jonah 1:4)

His way is in whirlwind and storm, and the clouds are the dust of his feet. *He rebukes the sea and makes it dry; he dries up all the rivers*.... (Nahum 1:3–4)

...and *I scattered them with a whirlwind* among all the nations that they had not known. Thus the land they left was desolate, so that no one went to and fro, and the pleasant land was made desolate. (Zech. 7:14)

...so that you may be sons of your Father who is in heaven. For he makes his sun rise on the evil and on the good, *and sends rain* on the just and on the unjust. (Matt. 5:45)

Yet he did not leave himself without witness, for he did good by *giving you rains* from heaven and fruitful seasons, satisfying your hearts with food and gladness. (Acts 14:17)

These various examples of divinely intended famine, drought, animal attacks, disease, birth defects, and death, as well as the biblical teaching of God's complete control over and use of the destructive powers of nature that bring about these things, provide ample biblical support for the view that these natural evils can indeed be traced back to the will of God. But it should be emphasized that although the vast majority of the cases mentioned above are clearly instances of *divine punishment or chastisement for sin*, the point of the above lists is *not* to support the idea that every instance or even most instances of these natural evils in the world are an individual punishment of some sort from God! The Bible repeatedly warns against the temptation to make that inference in any individual case. We are simply too ignorant to make a reliable guess.

We have already seen how Job's friends were mistaken in this respect when they wrongly attributed Job's sufferings to his sin (Job 42:7). Jesus's disciples were also mistaken when they speculated that the man born blind was that way because God was punishing either the man or his parents for their sin. Jesus flatly denies that explanation, and affirms a higher divine purpose in that case (John 9:1–3). Jesus sharply corrected first-century guessers who suspected, in specific cases, that some people suffered because they 'were worse sinners than' others (Luke 13:1–5). And when the pagan Maltese natives saw a poisonous viper slither out from a campfire and fasten itself to the apostle Paul's hand, they immediately concluded Paul was being punished by the gods for his sin. In this they were mistaken (Acts 28:3–6). Thus both Jews and non-Jews in the Bible repeatedly go wrong when they try to infer divine punishment from the mere existence of human suffering. (This obvious fact about our own ignorance will be explored further in the next chapter.) But what the above lists of verses establish is that *no one would go wrong in tracing natural evils back to the will of God.*

GOD'S SOVEREIGNTY OVER MORAL EVIL

Moral evil is significant pain and suffering in the world that is caused by free persons either intentionally or through culpable neglect of their responsibilities. These include such things as murder, adultery, disobedience to parents, rejecting wise counsel, and human hatred. As surprising as it may seem, the Bible presents God as having such meticulous control over the course of human history that each of the moral evils just named can be regarded as 'of the LORD.' Even as God doesn't merely permit nature to 'do its thing,' so he doesn't merely permit humans to 'do their thing.' Without erasing or suppressing the intentionality of creatures—and this includes their deliberations, their reasoning, their choosing between alternatives they consider and reflect upon—God's own intentionality stands above and behind the responsible choices of his creatures. In addition to the Sabeans' and Chaldeans' murder and theft (in the case of Job), Joseph's brothers betraying and selling their brother into slavery (in the case of Joseph), and the morally evil role of the Jewish leaders, Judas, and Pilate in the crucifixion of an innocent man (in the case of Jesus), here is just a selection of further examples of moral evil being 'from the LORD.'

Eli's sons' disobedience. Eli was a priest who had two sons who were also priests, Hophni and Phinehas (1 Sam. 1:3).

His sons 'were worthless men. They did not know the Lord' (2:12). Their regular practice was to steal for themselves the meat being offered by the Israelites at the tabernacle, something utterly contrary to God's commands to priests. 'Thus the sin of the young men was very great in the sight of the Lord, for the men treated the offering of the Lord with contempt' (2:17). Eli eventually rebuked his sons for this, but it was a case of parental concern that was 'too little, too late':

> And he said to them, 'Why do you do such things? For I hear of your evil dealings from all these people. No, my sons; it is no good report that I hear the people of the Lord spreading abroad. If someone sins against a man, God will mediate for him, but if someone sins against the Lord, who can intercede for him?' *But they would not listen to the voice of their father, for it was the will of the Lord to put them to death.* (1 Sam. 2:23–25)

While the sinful reaction of these wayward sons to their father's rebuke was entirely predictable ('But they would not listen to the voice of their father'), the explanation given for their sinful reaction is not ('for it was the will of the Lord to put them to death'). Hophni and Phinehas rejecting the admonishment and pleadings of their father was surely a sinful act on their part, bringing great grief to Eli. We would expect the passage to say that God eventually put them to death because of this sin. But in this case the Bible says the reverse: this sinful act happened *because* God desired to kill them. That is, there is an explanation for their not listening to their father, and it is grounded in the will of God rather than ultimately in the will of man. God planned to put them to death (1 Sam. 2:34), and he eventually did so by way of battle with the Philistines (1 Sam. 4:11). And because this was God's plan, Hophni and Phinehas did not listen to their father. If they had repented at this point, the singular judgment God was to promise could not have been carried out! None of this is meant to deny the accountability of the sons for their actions, only to underscore that their actions themselves were explainable in light of a higher purpose of God.

Samson's desire for a foreign wife. Samson was one of the last deliverers of Israel that God raised up in the period of the 'judges' (temporary leaders in the transitional period between Joshua's generalship and Saul's kingship). Israelites were forbidden from marrying non-Israelites, not for racial reasons but religious ones: pagan outsiders would corrupt and undermine the religious devotion of their Israelite spouses (Exod. 34:16; Deut. 7:3–4; cf. 1 Kings 11:1–8). But Samson sinfully desired a foreign wife for himself, contrary to God's command:

Samson went down to Timnah, and at Timnah he saw one of the daughters of the Philistines. Then he came up and told his father and mother, 'I saw one of the daughters of the Philistines at Timnah. Now get her for me as my wife.' But his father and mother said to him, 'Is there not a woman among the daughters of your relatives, or among all our people, that you must go to take a wife from the uncircumcised Philistines?' *But Samson said to his father, 'Get her for me, for she is right in my eyes.' His father and mother did not know that it was from the* Lord, for he was seeking an opportunity against the Philistines. At that time the Philistines ruled over Israel. (Judg. 14:1–4)

Even though this was a sinful request on the part of Samson, the Bible reveals something that Samson's parents couldn't possibly have discerned in their situation: Samson's request 'was from the Lord', to carry out God's larger purposes at that stage in Israel's history. The narrative never portrays Samson's request here as anything but sinful—it led to quite a few tragic events, involving much bloodshed and destruction. But presumably it was not a sin for God to so purpose Samson's sin in this situation.

Absalom, Rehoboam, and Amaziah rejecting wise counsel.
When King David's son Absalom conspired to seize the throne from his father, he entertained advice from his advisers as to what to do next. Ahithophel encouraged

Absalom to take action immediately to secure his throne, whereas Hushai counseled that Absalom delay and gather his forces first (2 Sam. 17:1–13). It is clear to the readers that Ahithophel's advice was far wiser, and should have been followed by Absalom if he desired to succeed, while Hushai's advice was a delaying tactic intended to help King David (Hushai's friend) escape from being struck down in battle. Nevertheless:

> Absalom and all the men of Israel said, 'The counsel of Hushai the Archite is better than the counsel of Ahithophel.' *For the LORD had ordained to defeat the good counsel of Ahithophel, so that the LORD might bring harm upon Absalom.* (2 Sam. 17:14)

Presumably it is a sin not to listen to wise counsel, as the book of Proverbs indicates multiple times (Prov. 11:14; 12:15; 13:10; 19:20). But Absalom's sinful failure here is explained by way of the higher purpose of God: 'For the LORD had ordained to defeat the good counsel of Ahithophel, so that the LORD might bring harm upon Absalom.'

Likewise when King David's grandson Rehoboam sought to establish his throne, he received advice from counselors both young and old. But Rehoboam followed the foolish advice of the young rather than the wise advice of the old (1 Kings 12:1–14), a decision that would eventually bring civil war and years of bloodshed to the land. But why did Rehoboam sin in this way?

> So the king did not listen to the people, *for it was a turn of affairs brought about by the* Lord *that he might fulfill his word,* which the Lord spoke by Ahijah the Shilonite to Jeroboam the son of Nebat. (1 Kings 12:15)

This 'turn of affairs'—the king refusing to heed wise counsel—was not only 'brought about by the Lord,' but was according to a particular purpose God had in mind: to 'fulfill his word, which the Lord spoke.' So God did not merely give a bare prediction of this event (1 Kings 11:11, 31). In addition, he subsequently brought about the (sinful) events that fulfilled his prediction (through responsible human agency, of course).

Finally, although Amaziah king of Judah had many battlefield victories, he eventually fell into idolatry (the worship of a created thing rather than God himself), and then in his pride he challenged Joash king of Israel to a completely unnecessary fight. Joash sought to dissuade him, '*but Amaziah would not listen, for it was of God*, in order that he might give them into the hand of their enemies, because they had sought the gods of Edom.' (2 Chron. 25:20) God's purpose was to punish Amaziah for his idolatry, and the pathway to that punishment involved God's planning that Amaziah would seek this foolish fight and spurn good counsel against it. The senseless battle, which involved the destruction of property and the taking of hostages (2 Chron. 25:21–24), could have been avoided if only Amaziah had listened. But his not listening 'was of God.'

Assassination. The rise and fall of kings in Israel and Judah (the north and south portions of the divided Israelite kingdom), and even on the broader world stage, was often accompanied by intrigue and devious plots. In this context, even assassinations were intended by God to come to pass:

> King Ahaziah being killed by Jehu: '*But it was ordained by God that the downfall of Ahaziah should come about through his going to visit Joram….* He searched for Ahaziah, and he was captured while hiding in Samaria, and *he was brought to Jehu and put to death.*' (2 Chron. 22:7, 9)

> King Sennacherib of Assyria being killed by his own sons: 'And the LORD sent an angel, who cut off all the mighty warriors and commanders and officers in the camp of the king of Assyria. So he returned with shame of face to his own land. And when he came into the house of his god, *some of his own sons struck him down there with the sword. So the LORD saved Hezekiah and the inhabitants of Jerusalem from the hand of Sennacherib king of Assyria* and from the

hand of all his enemies, and *he provided for them on every side.*'[3] (2 Chron. 32:21–22)

Adultery. After David commits adultery with Bathsheba and kills her husband Uriah the Hittite, God sends the prophet Nathan to rebuke him for his sin and pronounce his chastisement against him:

> 'Thus *says* the LORD, "Behold, *I will raise up evil against you out of your own house.* And I will take your wives before your eyes and give them to your neighbor, and he shall lie with your wives in the sight of this sun. For you did it secretly, but I will do this thing before all Israel and before the sun."' (2 Sam. 12:11–12)

The 'evil' (*rā'āh*) God promises to raise up against King David is the evil of David's concubines being given to his son Absalom to lie with, which is indeed what happened (2 Sam. 16:22). Concubinage is a form of marriage (cf. Judg. 19:9), which is why this episode was so odious to the Israelites (2 Sam. 16:21).

Human hatred.

> Egyptian hatred of the Israelites: 'Then Israel came to Egypt; Jacob sojourned in the land of Ham. And the LORD made

---

3   God saved Hezekiah king of Judah, and provided for the safety of his people, by way of this assassination.

his people very fruitful and made them stronger than their foes. *He turned their hearts to hate his people*, to deal craftily with his servants.' (Ps. 105:23–25)

Pharaoh's determination to keep the Israelites under harsh slavery: 'And the LORD said to Moses, "When you go back to Egypt, see that you do before Pharaoh all the miracles that I have put in your power. *But I will harden his heart, so that he will not let the people go.*"' (Exod. 4:21; cf. 7:3; 9:12; 10:1, 20, 27; 11:10; 14:4, 8; Rom. 9:17–18)

The Canaanites making war against the Israelites: 'But Sihon the king of Heshbon would not let us pass by him, *for the LORD your God hardened his spirit and made his heart obstinate*, that he might give him into your hand, as he is this day…. *Then Sihon came out against us*, he and all his people, to battle at Jahaz.' (Deut. 2:30, 32; cf. Num. 21:23–24)

The Canaanites making war against the Israelites: '*For it was the LORD's doing to harden their hearts that they should come against Israel in battle*, in order that they should be devoted to destruction and should receive no mercy but be destroyed, just as the LORD commanded Moses.' (Josh. 11:20)

The Syrian king making war against the Israelites: '*God also raised up as an adversary to him, Rezon* the son of Eliada…. *He was an adversary of Israel* all the days of Solomon, doing harm as Hadad did. *And he loathed Israel* and reigned over Syria.' (1 Kings 11:23, 25)

The Philistines making war against the Israelites: '*And the* Lᴏʀᴅ *stirred up against Jehoram the anger of the Philistines* and of the Arabians who are near the Ethiopians. *And they came up against Judah and invaded it* and carried away all the possessions they found that belonged to the king's house, and also his sons and his wives, so that no son was left to him except Jehoahaz, his youngest son.' (2 Chron. 21:16–17)

Gᴏᴅ's sᴏᴠᴇʀᴇɪɢɴᴛʏ ᴏᴠᴇʀ ᴀʟʟ ᴇᴠɪʟ

Should we universalize these particulars? It might be argued that it is both unwise and irresponsible to engage in hasty generalization, to infer from even this considerably extended list of examples that therefore God must intend and bring to pass all calamities, including all of those which trace back to the immoral decision-making of humans. But in addition to these particular texts about particular evils— and there has been a fairly large number of them in these past two chapters!—there are more 'universal' texts that seem to trace all calamities, all human decision-making, all events whatsoever, back to the will of God.

God's sovereignty over all calamity.

Consider the work of God: who can make straight *what he has made crooked?* In the day of prosperity (*tōv*) be joyful, and *in the day of adversity (rāʿāh)* consider: *God has made the one as well as the other,* so that man may not find out anything that will be after him. (Eccles. 7:13–14)

I form light and create darkness, *I make well-being (shālōm) and create calamity (rāʿ), I am the* LORD, *who does all these things.* (Isa. 45:7)

Who has spoken and it came to pass, unless the LORD has commanded it? *Is it not from the mouth of the Most High that good (tōv) and bad (rāʿāh) come?* (Lam. 3:37–38)

The implied answers to these last two rhetorical questions are: 'no one' and 'yes'. Nothing happens except if God has decreed it. Calamities (in general) and good things (in general) come from the Lord. There are no contextual qualifiers here, and we should be reluctant to arbitrarily impose them.

Is a trumpet blown in a city, and the people are not afraid? *Does disaster (rāʿāh) come to a city, unless the* LORD *has done it?* (Amos 3:6)

So according to these texts, God has made the day of *rāʿāh,* God creates *rāʿāh,* it is from his mouth that *rāʿāh* comes, and it is the Lord's doing that *rāʿāh* comes to a city.

God's sovereignty over all human decision-making.

The heart of man plans his way, but the LORD establishes his steps. (Prov. 16:9)

Many are the plans in the mind of a man, but it is the purpose of the LORD that will stand. (Prov. 19:21)

A man's steps are from the LORD; how then can man understand his way? (Prov. 20:24)

The king's heart is a stream of water in the hand of the LORD; he turns it wherever he will. (Prov. 21:1)

I know, O LORD, that the way of man is not in himself, that it is not in man who walks to direct his steps. (Jer. 10:23)

God's sovereignty over all events whatsoever.

Our God is in the heavens; he does all that he pleases. (Ps. 115:3)

The lot is cast into the lap, but its every decision is from the LORD. (Prov. 16:33)

…for I am God, and there is no other; I am God, and there is none like me, declaring the end from the beginning and from ancient times things not yet done, saying, 'My counsel shall stand, and I will accomplish all my purpose.' (Isa. 46:9–10)

And we know that for those who love God all things work together for good, for those who are called according to his purpose. (Rom. 8:28)

For from him and through him and to him are all things. To him be glory forever. Amen. (Rom. 11:36)

In him we have obtained an inheritance, having been predestined according to the purpose of him who works all things according to the counsel of his will…. (Eph. 1:11)

God works or accomplishes 'all things' (not just some things). And he effects them according to the purpose, intention, plan of his will. This is no afterthought, making the best of a bad situation after the fact. 'All things' are done according to the divine purpose. In fact, in this text Paul understands and accounts for the spiritual predestination of individuals in light of the broader, more general truth about God's providential plan for all things.

DEALING WITH THE GENERAL CONCLUSION ABOUT GOD'S RELATION TO EVIL

What are the relevant alternatives for Christians? In examining the Bible my strategy so far has been to go from many particular truths (about moral evils and natural evils) to some general truths (about all evils and events whatsoever).

Doing so reinforces the general conclusion that the divine intentionality stands above and behind *all* the evils in the world (whether natural or moral). The general passages just considered are crucial to the case, since without them it is open to the reader to say, 'Well, this is just a series of examples. How do we know that God's intentionality is behind *every* calamity? Maybe we should reach the *opposite* conclusion. It's precisely because God mentions his intentionality only *once in a while* in the Bible that we see that he only relates to evil like this once in a while. And he only exercises this kind of control once in a while.'

But once we consider these more general texts about divine providence, we see that God actually gives us a broader vision. God speaks about the specifics in individual cases so that we can repeatedly *see* that it *does* work out in individual cases. At the same time, he assures us of a more general perspective in other texts, in light of which the otherwise surprising, particular texts make more sense. When you put these two perspectives together, it is a very strong case that we are to take the particulars as instances of the more general view taught elsewhere. In fact, sometimes the particular and general perspectives come together *in the same passage*, thus illuminating each other. Notice that in Ephesians 1:11, the apostle Paul teaches a doctrine of particular, individual predestination: 'In him we have obtained an inheritance, having been predestined....' But he explains this particular truth as a consequence of God's general providence over all things: '… according to the purpose of him who works all things according to the counsel of his will.' Likewise, in Romans chapter 9 Paul situates his understanding of individual election and judgment (vv. 6-18) within a larger doctrine of God's role as the potter and our status as the clay (vv. 19–23).

As far as I can tell, the only reason to resist generalizing God's intentionality to all evils is because of an 'in principle' argument: there must be something wrong *in principle* with the idea that God intends that *any* evil come to pass. Such an argument might be made by Christians (those seeking a fundamentally different solution to the problem of evil), or by critics of Christianity (who might regard the biblical teaching I have outlined as ultimately making the problem of evil *worse*).

But (addressing myself to the Christian for a moment), is it at all plausible to think that there is something wrong *in principle* with the intentionality view? If that were the case, then *not a single one* of these numerous biblical texts have been interpreted correctly, and that is highly unlikely! You can dodge a few pebbles but you can't dodge an avalanche! Christians should ask themselves: could it really be the case that God *didn't* intend the cross, that he didn't plan that the innocent Jesus would be put to death? Could it be that, with respect to what befell Joseph, God *didn't* intend it for good because he didn't intend it at all? Could it be that in Job's case the Lord *didn't* take away? Or is the idea that God can only intend natural evil as *punishment* for sins, but not for any other purpose? Not only is this refuted by John 9:1–3, but we'll see in the next chapter that it is woefully short-sighted to so arbitrarily restrict the range of purposes God might have for these kinds of evils. Finally, even if only *some* of these passages have been interpreted correctly, it follows that certain approaches to the problem of evil are in trouble. In particular, those approaches that routinely deny the divine intentionality with respect to *any* evils: the free-will theodicy and natural law theodicy. If I'm right, then the alternatives available to Christians are far more restricted than may appear at first glance, and the Greater-Good theodicy may be the only game in town. I'll have more to say about this in chapter 5.

What about the goodness of God? Still, the preceding lists of verses might initially strike readers (including critics of Christianity) as fundamentally depressing. 'I didn't know that God was connected to so many kinds of evils in the world! What about the *goodness* of God!' But reading these passages in their context enables us to see them in their proper perspective. God both declares and exercises his control over these evils *to bring to pass his good purposes*. In quite a few of the passages about particular events, God is fulfilling his promise to those who love and trust him that he will protect them from their enemies. Or he is displaying his unrivalled power over the natural and human realms to provide a firm basis for trusting him, to indicate that he knows what he is doing and can bring it to pass. Or he is displaying his justice in the face of many human sins so that we can more easily believe that he will justly and with finality visit the rest of human sin. Or he is reminding us that life is a precious gift and privilege from him that can be removed at any moment, thus encouraging us to be thankful for the life we have received. For these and many more reasons, these passages should lead us to marvel at the *goodness* of God, even though they relate God to various evils.

If one wants direct biblical support for the view that God is sovereign over all *goods* as well as all evils, passages are not hard to find.

> The Lord is gracious and merciful, slow to anger and abounding in steadfast love. The Lord is good to all, and his mercy is over all that he has made…. The Lord is faithful in all his words and kind in all his works. (Ps. 145:8–9, 13)

> Every good gift and every perfect gift is from above, coming down from the Father of lights with whom there is no variation or shadow due to change. (James 1:17)

> God is love. (1 John 4:8, 16)

In focusing so much of this chapter on God's intentionality behind *evils*, I do not mean to neglect the equally important truth that God intends all the goods as well. However, this book is about the problem of evil, and defending a Greater-Good theodicy *requires* showing that God has enough control over the evils of the world to pull it off, as it were. Only a God who has this kind of meticulous control over evils as a means to great goods can *ensure* that the great goods he aims at will in fact come to pass. God is not merely wishing that creation turns out for the good, and wishing that we'll join him in his risky wishing project. He is far more worthy of our worship than that! Anyone can start a wishing project and ask others to join him. Far grander is the thought that one who is *this* exalted and majestic, who can bring to pass *all* of his settled purposes, invites us to be free from our sin and guilt and inherit an enduring kingdom which we do not deserve but which he can guarantee us with certainty.

PRIMARY AND SECONDARY CAUSALITY

The distinction itself. It is time to draw and defend a distinction that not only preserves but argues for God's moral innocence in the midst of his sovereignly intending evils for good. It is the distinction between primary and secondary causality. (This is sometimes described as the difference between ultimate and proximate causality, or between remote and near causality. These three pairs of terms are attempts to get at the same distinction.) Simply put, *it is not a sin to ordain that there be sin.* It is not evil to ordain that evil be. Indeed, if the greatest good was only obtainable by way of the existence of evil, it is clearly *good* that there be evil. If God is so meticulously sovereign over evils, wouldn't it be wrong for him *not* to work them out to a greater good? But to do that would require his intention that these evils be the means of that good.

The distinction can be illustrated by way of the Job, Joseph, and Jesus passages considered in the previous chapter. In each case we had one set of events but two sets of intentions with respect to those events (human intentions and divine intentions). Thus in each case we had sinful persons on the scene committing the sins and therefore perpetrating the moral evil for which they were accountable: the Sabeans, the Chaldeans, Satan, Joseph's brothers, Potiphar's wife, the Jewish leaders, Judas, Pilate, and so on. Their causality is to be recognized and not explained away. But God is not to be listed as one of the sinners at the scene of the crime, acting with evil intentions. In the case of *moral* evil at least, there is *always* a human (or fallen angelic) agent who is the secondary, proximate, near cause of the sin in space and time.

What does God do? And then there is God. What does he do? Fundamentally, God uses means to bring about his chosen ends. The various evils occur in the world because of creaturely decisions, but the *ultimate* reason these evils occur is not because of creaturely decisions, but because of divine decisions. Thus Job's family, servants, animals, and health are said to be 'taken away' by the Lord, and this evil is 'brought upon him' by the Lord and is 'from God.' And so their earthly causes are the *means* by which God does these things. Likewise, Joseph's sufferings are said to be 'intended' by God for good, and so their earthly causes are the *means* by which God realizes his good intentions, and thereby he 'sent a man ahead of them, Joseph.' God's 'hand' and 'plan' 'predestined to take place' the sufferings of Jesus, such that he was 'delivered up according to the definite plan' of God. But Jesus was 'crucified and killed *by* the hands of lawless men', and so the means by which God's plan comes to pass were 'Herod and Pontius Pilate, along with the Gentiles and the peoples of Israel.'

So the distinction between primary and secondary causality is in part the affirmation that God uses means to bring about his chosen ends. Sometimes these means are responsible persons committing moral evils, and sometimes these means are simply the powers of impersonal objects and forces bringing about natural evils. A remarkable example of primary and secondary causality coming together is found in the Old Testament narrative of the death of Saul, who was rejected by God as king of Israel because of his sin, and who was eventually wounded in battle by the Philistines. Saul then commits suicide when his armor-bearer won't finish the job:

> Then Saul said to his armor-bearer, 'Draw your sword and thrust me through with it, lest these uncircumcised come and mistreat me.' But his armor-bearer would not, for he feared greatly. Therefore Saul took his own sword and fell upon it. And when his armor-bearer saw that Saul was dead, he also fell upon his sword and died. Thus Saul died; he and his three sons and all his house died together. (1 Chron. 10:4–6)

Who killed Saul? The answer according to this passage is perfectly straightforward: Saul killed Saul, by deliberately falling on his own sword and committing suicide. But to leave the answer there would be only telling one side of the story, privileging the secondary causality of humans to the exclusion of the primary causality of God. For the narrative goes on to say:

> So Saul died for his breach of faith. He broke faith with the Lord in that he did not keep the command of the Lord, and also consulted a medium, seeking guidance. He did not seek guidance from the Lord. Therefore the Lord put him to death and turned the kingdom over to David the son of Jesse. (1 Chron. 10:13–14)

Who killed Saul? The answer according to *this* passage is also perfectly straightforward: 'Therefore the LORD put him to death.' That is, God killed Saul. A more concise combining of the teaching of both passages is to say that God killed Saul *by means of* Saul killing Saul. The moral evil of Saul's suicide—that is, Saul's responsible human agency—was the means by which God put him to death. But saying that doesn't convert two causal claims into one. It doesn't mean that God *didn't* put him to death. 'Killing' is one of the most consequential, causally efficacious verbs in the entire Bible, and God killed Saul. If you 'put someone to death' you don't merely allow him to die. You do something. So primary causality and secondary causality are at work in bringing about the end of Saul's earthly life, and the account would be incomplete if we left out either kind of causality.

Likewise, with the death of Jesus. Clearly, the Roman soldiers put Jesus to death. But according to the prophet Isaiah's marvelous prediction of the death of Christ, the Bible also says that God did it: 'we esteemed him stricken, smitten by God, and afflicted… it was the will of the LORD to crush him; he has put him to grief' (Isa. 53:4, 10). Indeed, we may have a *third* cause of Jesus's death, Jesus himself: 'I lay down my life that I may take it up again. No one takes it from me, but I lay it down of my own accord' (John 10:17–18).

Primary causality without secondary causality. God does not always do things in the indirect way depicted in the passage about Saul. He is free to bring things about directly, quite apart from responsible, secondary means. This seems to be the case just three chapters after the Saul narrative, when Uzzah foolishly touched the Ark of the Covenant despite God's clearly commanding it should *never* be touched (Num. 4:15). In response: 'the anger of the Lord was kindled against Uzzah, and he struck him down because he put out his hand to the ark, and he died there before God' (1 Chron. 13:10). No secondary causality here needed—this was a miracle precisely because God *didn't* use means. Uzzah just dropped dead. Or again, when Uzziah king of Judah presumptuously grasped at the spiritual privileges of the priests, 'and entered the temple of the Lord to burn incense on the altar of incense' (2 Chron. 26:16), the Bible says that 'leprosy broke out on his forehead in the presence of the priests in the house of the Lord, by the altar of incense… because the Lord had struck him' (2 Chron. 26:19-20). Again, no secondary causality needed; the leprosy simply appeared.

Of course, some natural evils *are* likely brought about by secondary causes. The blindness of the 'man blind from birth' in John 9:1-3 was presumably the result of a genetic defect (or maternal infection during pregnancy), though Jesus says that behind that blindness was a divine purpose: 'that the works of God might be displayed in him.' It follows that for some natural evils secondary causality is present (the man born blind) whereas for other natural evils secondary causality is absent (Uzzah's death, Uzziah's leprosy). But notice that whereas some natural evils may be brought about without secondary causes, and therefore miraculously and directly, moral evils are *only* brought about by way of responsible secondary causes and never without them, that is, never directly. In this way God remains blameless. The sinful intentions of creatures are never *his* intentions. God is not Joseph's brothers.

Avoiding misleading models. Can we say more about *how* God causally relates to various events? Is there more to be said? I would like there to be! But causation is a notoriously difficult concept to analyze, philosophically speaking. The peer-reviewed *Stanford Encyclopedia of Philosophy* (online) has at least ten separate entries on the topic of 'causation,' and the entry on 'The Metaphysics of Causation' distinguishes at least six important questions about the nature of causes, effects, and causal relations, and then notes that 'Philosophers have, of course, disagreed over all of these questions.' Perhaps then, the Anglican theologian Austin Farrer was on to something when, in his book on *Faith and Speculation*, he expressed skepticism about the means of the divine causation, saying that it is essentially hidden from us: 'Both the divine and the human actions remain real and therefore free in the union between them; not knowing the modality of the divine action we cannot pose the problem of their mutual relation.'

That is, we are ignorant of the precise extent to which divine causation is like human causation. The truth of the matter is that *we don't know* how God exercises his primary causality through secondary, instrumental causes. Presumably it's somewhat more inscrutable than a Mafia don ordering a hit! A divine hand didn't come out of heaven and push Saul down on his sword, or slap the Egyptians silly until they burned with hatred toward the Israelites. Secret voices weren't whispering in the ears of Joseph's brothers, 'Do it! Do it!' The Roman soldiers weren't dragged along by a Death Star-like tractor beam and forced to drive in the nails.

Of course, there surely *is* an analogy between the mode of divine action and human action, such that they are both causal in nature. (Why else the blunt and repeated biblical language about the divine intentions behind evil human plots, and various ill acts being 'of the LORD'?) But there isn't an *identity* between the two types of action. So there is no need to describe divine causality as a copy of mundane (that is, earthly) causation, and it would be misleading to do so. After all, we don't understand and cannot imitate God's *creation* of all things out of nothing. All of *our* causation is by way of pre-existing materials. It's therefore to be expected that God's causation in *providence* is equally inexplicable to us. One thing we shouldn't do is understand the ultimate/ proximate causality distinction in terms of mere 'distance,' or links on a chain, such that God's causality is just an 'earlier' link in the chain, and our causality comes 'later.' In some way God's causal activity ensures the whole chain *and* our responsible exercise of our powers as links in that chain. The other thing we cannot do is turn two causal claims into one (and insist on either a divine cause *or* a human cause, but not both).

Does this leave us with a certain measure of mystery, with things 'hard to understand' (2 Pet. 3:16)? Yes, but it locates that mystery in exactly the right place. Does this confession of ignorance on the part of the Christian contradict the Bible or violate the laws of logic? How? I have in fact come close to the topic of the next chapter. We cannot on our own discern either the content of God's ultimate purposes or the method of his ultimate causality in any situation. Does admitting this somehow undermine the goal of defending the Christian faith? No, it simply presents to the world a God whose ways and methods are to some extent mysterious to us. But this is *already* a commitment of good Christian theology, simply with respect to creation, quite apart from questions about evil. On the question of God's creative purpose, *why* did God create the range of creatures he did, or the number of planets and galaxies he did? We have no idea, and it would be foolish to speculate. On the question of

God's creative method, *how* did God create material things from no pre-existing material whatsoever? Again, we have no idea, and even the most advanced scientific models of the Big Bang don't posit a universe coming from absolutely *nothing* (there is at the very least the quantum vacuum, and laws pertaining to it). Such models therefore don't and can't capture what God actually did in that first moment. So why would Christians want to hide the mysteriousness of God's *providence* from unbelievers, when the basic doctrine of *creation* we want unbelievers to accept already reveals him to be mysterious, at least in part? What matters is not banishing all mystery from our conception of God, but locating that mystery in the right place, in the place we would *expect* to find it. How an infinite, spiritual being brings about events in the space-time continuum would seem to be a good candidate.

Is God doing evil that good may come? (answering the objection from Romans 3:8)

The passage itself. What then of the apparent moral conflict between the 'intentionality view' of God's relation to evil, and the teaching of Romans 3:8? In that passage Paul has been arguing that God is righteous to inflict his wrath on unrighteous sinners, for that is what our sins deserve: his judgment. Thus, our *unrighteousness* provides God with an occasion to show his *righteousness* to the world, by way of his judgment. One might say that our unrighteousness is therefore a *means* to God's showing people that he is righteous. Paul's argument here, far from denying any means-end connection between our unrighteousness in sin and God's righteousness in judgment, *presupposes* such a connection. That in itself is instructive, given the main argument of this chapter. But Paul continues:

> But if our unrighteousness serves to show the righteousness of God, what shall we say? That God is unrighteous to inflict wrath on us? (I speak in a human way.) By no means! For then how could God judge the world? But if through my lie God's truth abounds to his glory, why am I still being condemned as a sinner? And why not do evil that good may come?—as some people slanderously charge us with saying. Their condemnation is just. (Rom. 3:5–8)

Paul says that there are people who conclude from the fact that 'through my lie God's truth abounds to his glory,' that therefore I shouldn't be 'condemned as a sinner.' These people even tell the lie ('slanderously charge us with saying') that Paul's teaching is: 'why not do evil that good may come?' In response, Paul says of such people: 'Their condemnation is just.' Paul entirely rejects the idea that this is anything he has taught, or is even an implication of his teaching.

Its moral principle. So we can lay it down as a fundamental moral principle: *no one may do evil that good may come.* But isn't this exactly what God is doing in the Greater-Good theodicy? And doesn't this mean that any attempt to endorse such a theodicy as a solution to the problem of evil only makes the problem *worse*? Are we not making God evil in order to reconcile him with evil? Are we not giving up his perfect goodness?

No, we are not. It *is* a fundamental moral principle that no one is allowed to *do evil* that good may come. But on the ultimate/proximate causality distinction, God isn't *doing evil* when he ordains that evil be. Rather, he is at worst ensuring that *human agents* do evil, and he is ensuring this *to realize good purposes* that would not otherwise come to pass. As we saw explicitly in the Job, Joseph, and Jesus passages, and implicitly in the others, the difference between the divine and human intentions makes all the difference in the world. So God is not the agent who *does* the evil. Humans are. God is the agent who *ordains* that the evil shall be.

Now, it may be that the critic is deriving a different principle from Romans 3:8, one not actually taught in the passage: it is evil, immoral, or otherwise morally suspect to *ordain suffering* that good may come. But first, this principle is false, since we already accept that it is good to ordain suffering—at least within very narrow limits—for the limited kinds of discipline we impose for the rearing

117

of children or the reformation of criminals. (Or consider the dentist example given in chapter 1.) And second, what would be immoral would be to ordain suffering when we don't have the *right* to impose it, or when we don't have the *knowledge or power* to ensure that suffering works for good. And while this clearly seems to apply in the human context, it doesn't in the divine one.

It is not evil to ordain that evil be, especially if one has the requisite knowledge and power to ensure the greater good (having knowledge to consider relevant alternatives, and having power to assure that evils will not be in vain with respect to providential purposes). We humans have neither the knowledge nor the power to do these things— and rarely the right—and so it would be positively immoral for us to ordain suffering that good may come. (Again, except within very narrow limits, such as the very limited kinds of discipline we impose for the rearing of children or the reformation of criminals.) But if God has the right to impose suffering, and the requisite knowledge and power to ensure greater goods out of it, it would not only *not be evil* for God to so ordain suffering, it would be *positively good* for him to do so. The Romans 3:8 passage is forbidding doing evil that good may come; it is not forbidding bringing about suffering to ensure a greater good. Even we are permitted to do the latter within limits, and God has considerably greater leeway here.

A threefold distinction. So let's distinguish three things: (1) doing evil, (2) ordaining the existence of significant pain and suffering, and (3) ordaining the existence of the free human choices which bring about significant pain and suffering. The first is impossible for God and forbidden to man: God *cannot* do this and humans *should not* do this. Nothing in the Greater-Good theodicy requires otherwise. The second is permissible for both God and man, within limits. There must be a good purpose for the suffering, and this good purpose must be matched with the right to impose the suffering, and also matched with adequate knowledge and power to accomplish the good purpose by way of the suffering. The third is both possible and permissible for God but strictly impossible for man. *God* might know how to 'ordain free human choices,' but we don't! This is simply beyond our causality.

Romans 3:8 is talking about the first thing. This chapter has been talking about God's doing the second and third things. Thus, solving the problem of evil by attributing the second and third things to God does nothing to undermine the teaching of this passage. These points will go a long way toward licensing the Greater-Good theodicy as something Christians can and ought to use in response to the problem of evil.

Summary of main points

- Christians are licensed to use the Greater-Good theodicy as a *general* response to the problem of evil, for the passages examined in this chapter show that the relation God sustains to evil in the Job, Joseph, and Jesus passages is not an anomaly, but part and parcel of a more general view the Bible takes on the subject, with respect to both natural and moral evil.

- While natural evil comes from how 'nature goes on'— being caused by impersonal objects and forces quite independently of *human* choices—the Bible presents multitudes of examples of God intentionally bringing about these types of events (rather than being someone who merely permits nature to 'do its thing' on its own).

- God's own intentionality stands above and behind the responsible choices of his creatures, without erasing or suppressing their intentionality, deliberations, reasoning, and choosing between the alternatives they consider and reflect upon.

- The distinction between primary and secondary causality not only preserves but argues for God's moral innocence in the midst of his sovereignly intending evils for good.

- The Greater-Good theodicy is not a case of God 'doing evil that good may come.' It is not evil to ordain that evil be, especially if one has the requisite knowledge and power to ensure the greater good, and the right to impose the suffering.

4

Limiting the Greater-Good Theodicy: The Inscrutability of God's Purposes

FOUR KINDS OF GREATER-GOOD THEODICY

According to the Greater-Good theodicy, the pain and suffering in God's world play a necessary role in bringing about greater goods that could not be brought about except for the presence of that pain and suffering. The world would be worse off without that pain and suffering, and so God is justified in pursuing the good by these means. But this is a very general claim. While we have come to see more clearly the kinds of 'pain and suffering' there are in God's world (natural evil and moral evil), as well as God's sovereignty over them, little has been said about the 'greater goods' that God aims at by way of them. What are they? And how do they depend upon the various natural and moral evils in the world? As we'll see, the Greater-Good theodicy is a kind of wide-ranging 'umbrella' under which more specific theodicies can flourish. These tend to describe more fully the greater goods God aims at, and their connections with evils. In this chapter, we'll look at four such theodicies: punishment, soul-building, pain-as-God's-megaphone, and higher-order goods. In punishment God displays his justice. In soul-building he displays his goodness. In pain-as-God's-megaphone he displays his mercy. And in higher-order goods he aims at goods that are good precisely because they respond to and overcome the evils of the world.

The main argument of this chapter will be that while each of these theodicies seems promising, each also has significant limitations. None of them is a 'one size fits all' explanation for all evils. Because of built-in limitations to their explanatory scope, or because the Bible indicates that they are limited in application, and also because of our cognitive limitations as human beings, it is next to impossible to confidently 'rule in' any one of these theodicies as the likely explanation for any case of natural or moral evil we see in the world. In fact, the Bible itself encourages this skeptical view! But by similar reasoning, it is next to impossible to confidently 'rule out' the application of any one of these theodicies to a case of evil. (Unlike the theodicies to be considered in the next chapter, any one of these theodicies could be conceivably applied to moral evil *or* natural evil.) Since the critic of Christianity who is a proponent of the problem of evil bears the burden of proving his premises, there now seems little hope of his proving premise 2: 'A perfectly good being *would* prevent evil as far as he can.' For perhaps God has a good reason for permitting the evil he does permit, and one or more of these theodicies is his reason in any particular case. The critic would have to show that no theodicy *could* apply to it, to support his claim that a good God *would* prevent it. Since the critic cannot do this, the conclusion of the problem of evil is without support, and evil is no longer any reason to reject God's existence. (Of course, someone's *personal experience of evil* may continue to incline him or her to disbelief in God, but that is a pastoral rather than an intellectual challenge to Christianity, and Christians should be sensitive to it.)

PUNISHMENT (GOD DISPLAYING HIS JUDGMENT)

The punishment theodicy says that *suffering is a result of God's just punishment of evildoers*. It is an objectively good thing that God judges sin, as God's holding men accountable for their sin both upholds God's justice and reveals that justice to the world. It is to God's glory that he judges rather than overlooks sin. The idea that God can bring pain and suffering as his just judgment on sinners goes back to Genesis 3, in which God curses humans and the earth because of Adam and Eve's disobedience to him (vv. 14–19). It is because of this sin that 'death spread to all men' (Rom. 5:12), for 'the wages of sin is death' (Rom. 6:23). And God's curse doesn't just afflict humans but also the rest of the world they live in, which means that even 'the creation was subjected to futility' and has a 'bondage to corruption' (Rom. 8:20–21). The result is a world that, under God's just governance, is liable to produce quite a bit of awful suffering for the sinners who inhabit it.

If death is God's just judgment for sin, then presumably anything that stops short of death could be punishment for sin as well. As we saw in the last chapter, the Bible represents God as bringing about a wide range of natural evil as his punishment for people's sins. These include famine, drought, animal attacks, disease, and even death itself. Earthquakes, whirlwinds, and tempests can also occur as divine judgment (Isa. 29:5–6; Ezek. 38:19; Rev. 6:12; 11:13; 16:18). Beyond this, moral evil can be included under the punishment theodicy, for several cases of moral evil considered in the last chapter—including rejecting wise counsel, assassination, adultery, and human hatred—were each the means of God's just judgment on the individuals involved. In fact, Paul says more generally that God gives people over to further sin *as* punishment on them for their earlier sin.[1]

---

1   See the threefold repetition of 'God gave them up' in the wide-ranging list of sins noted in Romans 1:24–32. Here sin is both the reason for punishment and a form of the punishment itself.

So the punishment theodicy has ample biblical support (unlike, say, the theodicies we'll look at in the next chapter). But it can't be a way to explain *every* case of natural and moral evil. At the very least, if the evils of punishment are a response to human sin, then they cannot explain the very first sin (Adam's sin). For God permits Adam's sin as a means of punishing... who, exactly? Satan, the fallen angel who tempted Adam and Eve to sin? Then we ask again: God permits Satan's sin as a means of punishing... who, exactly? And now the regress ends; there are no other candidates. So the punishment theodicy can't explain *all* evil as God's punishment on prior sin.

The book of Job imposes another limitation on the punishment theodicy. God makes quite explicit in the prologue to the book that Job's suffering *wasn't* the result of his own evildoing. If anything, the dialogue between God and Satan in Job 1–2 reveals that Job was selected for suffering because of his faithfulness. In fact, in the relevant biblical narratives, neither Job nor Joseph nor Jesus suffer because of their sins. We also saw that neither the blind man's blindness (John 9:1–3) nor the poisonous snake attacking Paul (Acts 28:1–6) were punishment for sin.[2]

---

2   In Luke 13:1–5, Jesus doesn't deny that the deaths were punishment for sin; what he denies is that they suffered because they 'were worse sinners than' others.

So the Bible teaches that the punishment theodicy isn't a total explanation of evil in the world, which means that Christians shouldn't attempt to use this theodicy *comprehensively*. Beyond this, what about animal (non-human) suffering? The fawn in the forest fire can't be suffering for its sins, can it? It doesn't have any sins.

SOUL-BUILDING (GOD DISPLAYING HIS GOODNESS)

The soul-building theodicy says that *God's painful providences come into our lives to do us good, namely, to shape our character and lead us from self-centeredness to other-centeredness.* We don't start off life in this way at all, but rather as self-centered little babies who care only for ourselves. But pain and suffering can shape us in this better direction, promoting character development that leads us to be more loving, patient, and merciful to others (in this way coming to imitate God himself, which is a great good). On this view, suffering is a kind of regimen for our souls that is analogous to a physical regimen one would go through in a gymnasium. It is no accident that the English word 'discipline' applies in both contexts. In the gym, athletes learn physical discipline that promotes their physical success. In the home, parents discipline their children to promote their spiritual success. And not only is *literal* physical discipline from loving parents a theme in the book of Proverbs (10:13; 13:24; 22:15;

23:13-24; 29:15), but God's fatherly *spiritual* discipline of his children is a theme in the New Testament (Heb. 12:5–11, which quotes Prov. 3:11–12). In this way, God works painful circumstances for good in our lives.

The soul-building theodicy is grounded by the repeated exhortation in the New Testament that we should submit to the painful trials that God often brings, for God intends to do us spiritual good by them (Rom. 5:3–5; 2 Cor. 4:17; James 1:2–4; 1 Pet. 1:6–7). This last passage is quite instructive:

> In this you rejoice, though now for a little while, if necessary, you have been grieved by various trials, so that the tested genuineness of your faith—more precious than gold that perishes though it is tested by fire—may be found to result in praise and glory and honor at the revelation of Jesus Christ (1 Pet. 1:6-7).

On Peter's view, it may be '*necessary*' for us to be 'grieved by various trials'! The idea seems to be that the perseverance of Christian believers is so important for the praise and glory of God, and the faith by which they persevere is so valuable, that God may deem it necessary that they suffer so that their faith is tested and thereby strengthened. In this way their actually gaining the hoped-for heaven depends upon the sufferings of their trials.

Finally, even Jesus was made 'perfect through suffering' (Heb. 2:10), not because he had any self-centeredness to get rid of, but because his suffering opened up to him more and more opportunities to obey God for who he was rather than for the earthly goods that could be received from him. That is, over his lifetime and culminating in the cross, Jesus was enabled more and more to express his loyalty to his heavenly Father in the midst of adversity. His resisting the temptations of Satan in the wilderness (Matt. 4:1–11), which was surely a 'trial' in his life, fitted him to be an intercessor who is sympathetic to the weaknesses of those who trust in him (Heb. 4:14–16).

But can *every* pain and suffering we or anyone else suffer be placed into this category, as something intended by God to shape or develop our character in some way? Presumably not, since we're now familiar with the lengthy list of Bible verses that seem to support *another* theodicy, namely, the punishment theodicy. If we're right that those passages reveal various evils as *punishments* of some sort, it doesn't seem possible to generalize the soul-building theodicy to all evils. (Unless one and the same evil can be punishment for one person and a source of soul-building for another, a possibility that shouldn't be overlooked.) Beyond this, we seem to have ample reason for thinking that soul-building *doesn't* occur in many cases of suffering. The businessman isn't humbled by his failures; rather, he grows more bitter. The cancer patient doesn't learn to depend upon God more and count her blessings; she takes up Buddhism and renounces any personal conception of God instead. The mugging makes the victim fearful and paranoid rather than independent and self-reliant. We might put the point by saying that if soul-building *is* God's aim in all suffering, then it looks like he often misses the mark. It doesn't always seem to be 'worked together' for this good. And again we return to animal (non-human) suffering. Are we to imagine the fawn in the forest fire undergoing character development of some sort? Presumably not.

Pain-as-God's-megaphone (God displaying his mercy)

In his book *The Problem of Pain*, C. S. Lewis argues that *pain is God's megaphone to get our attention*. This is particularly needed if someone simply doesn't care about God at all. Perhaps he is devoted to the baubles of the world: money, fame, success, pleasure. *If* in fact no sinner will be delivered from the wrath to come unless he humbles himself, repents of his sin, and places his faith in the Lord Jesus for salvation, what will become of the one who simply doesn't care about spiritual things? God will not *coerce* us to come to him, in a way that utterly bypasses our capacities for rational reflection and deliberation. But he may use very difficult circumstances to wake us up from our devotion to the world, so that we would reflect upon and consider the life to come. Painful providences may be the means God uses to get our attention and lead us to consider our dependence on him and our obligation to seek him.

Paul says that 'God's kindness is meant to lead you to repentance' (Rom. 2:4). The idea in this theodicy is that God's *severity* can lead us to repentance as well. Imagine that we are addicted to God's blessings and we take no thought of the giver, God himself. But when these are taken away, with a sharpness and painfulness we did not anticipate, we suddenly realize that our life is relatively short, that it has been filled with good things and opportunities we didn't earn, and that—if we were honest with ourselves—we don't deserve. Whom should we thank? Whom should we serve? And what about my guilt over having lived for myself all this time? How do I get rid of that? The vanities of earth have been drowning out God's voice, but the megaphone of God's pain is finally heard above the din. To switch the metaphor, our blessings are removed, and in the silence of their absence, God's voice is heard.

There is surely a biblical basis for this theodicy. God's people in the Old Testament were often led astray by idolatry (the worship of a created thing rather than God himself). Whole generations seemed to depart from God altogether. But God in his mercy sent a series of judgments announced by his prophets for the purpose of awakening repentance in them. And this is precisely the alternative theodicy Jesus hints at when he *rules out* the punishment theodicy in the case of 'the Galileans whose blood Pilate had mingled with their sacrifices' and 'those eighteen on whom the tower in Siloam fell and killed them' (Luke 13:1, 4). Yes, those individuals have died, but there is nothing we can do about them now. What about Jesus's hearers, the ones who are so concerned about God's punishment on others? Are *they* ready to die? God's readiness to end any life at any moment should lead them to ask this question of themselves. Jesus regards these sobering events as a *warning* to his hearers that the whole world will be judged on the final day, for he tells them twice: 'But unless you repent, you will all likewise perish' (Luke 13:3, 5). The megaphone has sounded.

Still, this can't be a universal theodicy that explains all evils. Christians have already repented of their sins and placed their faith in Jesus. Why would *they* need pain in order to start a relationship with God? And for the rest of mankind, what about pain that seems to go far beyond what is needed in order to get their attention? Perhaps the first year of cancer led us to consider God, and definitely got our attention; what were the next three years for?

Some might posit animal (non-human) suffering as an exception to this theodicy, even as it seems to be an exception to the previous two theodicies. Here I am not so sure. Perhaps we need to see *their* suffering as well, in order to turn to God. Their pains are an eloquent testimony to us that we live in a deeply messed-up world, perhaps one that is cursed. How awful is that curse, how awful must be the thing that called it forth, if even the animals suffer, these sentient creatures capable of pain but who do not know right from wrong! But at the same time something in us cries out that it *ought not* to be this way. Recognizing this as evidence that we do live in a fallen world, and wondering how it can be set right, how our own lives can be set right, may be just the means God uses to awaken us to a spiritual perspective on our real needs. Maybe. But again the question returns, 'Why *so much* animal suffering?' Wouldn't we still know the world was cursed, if there were just half the animal suffering there is now? So for these reasons the pain-as-God's-megaphone theodicy has significant but limited explanatory scope.

HIGHER-ORDER GOODS (GOD AIMING AT GOODS THAT ARE GOOD PRECISELY BECAUSE THEY RESPOND TO AND OVERCOME THE EVILS OF THE WORLD)

The higher-order goods theodicy says that *at least some goods can't exist apart from evils because they are defined with reference to those evils*. The good just is a response to the evil, or even an overcoming of the evil. The good is 'higher-order' because it incorporates 'lower-order' evils in its very definition. In chapter 2, I mentioned that if it is a good thing to be brave in the face of battle, then there can't be such bravery without the danger of battle. Courage is a response to danger, sympathy is a response to human suffering, forgiveness is a response to sin, compassion is a response to human need, and patience is a response to adversity. In each of these, you can't have the first thing without the second. The idea isn't that these goods *have* to exist. God could decline to create a universe that had these goods, or even a universe at all. But if God wants these deep goods to be in his universe, because they make his universe far more valuable than it would otherwise be, then the evils will be there as well. For the goods wouldn't *be* the goods they are if they were a response to nothing.

It should be noted that it is no part of the higher-order goods theodicy to assert that the only 'higher-order' goods there may be are goods that are defined with respect to *evils*. Some higher-order goods are deep goods because their very nature is to be brought about by lesser or first-order *goods*. The higher-order good of children being mature and wise through parental instruction and influence depends upon the lower-order good of parents being faithful to train their children and teach them over time. The higher-order good of worshiping God according to one's knowledge of the truth about him depends upon the lower-order good of one's actually knowing the truth about him. The higher-order good of friendship depends upon the lower-order good of being the sort of person who is willing to enter into friendships. (This is one reason to distinguish between

God's aiming at greater goods and God's bringing good out of evil—not every greater good God aims at is a good that is brought about by *evil*.)

The higher-order goods theodicy may be the only theodicy in the list of four that can explain the very first sin, because perhaps God permitted it—that is, ordained it to occur through secondary causes rather than directly bringing it about—so that this would be a universe in which he would be known, worshiped, and glorified as redeemer as well as creator and providential sustainer. As we saw when discussing the moral evil of the cross in chapter 2, in Jesus's death are displayed the justice, love, grace, mercy, wisdom, and power of God, enabling us to worship God throughout eternity for being all these things as our Savior. Adam's sin and Jesus's cross may thereby secure the highest good for both God and man.

In fact, one could attempt to justify *all* evils, natural and moral, by way of two higher-order goods that require them: the display of God's justice, and the display of God's redemptive love. On this view, all natural evils display God's justice (because they are the means of divine punishment for sin), and all moral evils either enable the display of God's justice (because he punishes those who commit them) or enable the display of divine forgiveness (because he forgives those who commit them, if they repent of their sins and place their faith in Christ). Every evil, therefore, is explained with reference to divine justice or divine forgiveness, and so a universe without evil would be a universe without divine justice or forgiveness. It would still be a good universe in many ways, but not *as good* a universe as one with the evils. This view seems hard to accept, however, as the Bible indicates that at least some natural evils don't occur as punishment for sin (e.g., Job, or the man born blind), and some natural evils occur in the context of trials that are for soul-building or warnings-by-megaphone. (Indeed, the experience of *moral* evils could fall into these latter categories as well, when we suffer at the hands of others.)

Thus, each of these four theodicies face limitations to their explanatory scope, either intrinsically (because they have conceptual limits) or extrinsically (because God *tells us* they don't explain all evils).

CAN CHRISTIANS 'RULE IN' ONE OF THESE FOUR THEODICIES IN ANY PARTICULAR CASE?

Still, these limitations don't seem particularly damaging for someone who is committed to explaining all the evils in the world by way of theodicy. Yes, no single theodicy can explain *all* evils. But as long as *each* evil can be explained by *some* theodicy or other, then all is well. All evils are thereby 'covered,' as it were. But here we face a new challenge, deliberately delayed until now. For any case of significant pain and suffering in the world, do we know enough to 'rule in' the applicability of a theodicy to it? That is, do we know *both* of the following things? First, that the good obtained by the evil is a *weighty* enough good, so that it is 'worth it' in light of the evil that it requires? Second, that the good obtained by the evil *did require* the evil in question, and could not have been obtained without it? That the goods be both 'weighty' and 'dependent' were seen to be the two assumptions behind all successful theodicies in chapter 2.

Well, *can* we confidently make these ethical judgments about the scale of values, and these metaphysical judgments about the dependent structure of reality? Can we *know* that forgiveness is so valuable that it outweighs cases of mass shooting? Can we *know* that someone's character development (either mine or another's) outweighs the wiping out of their entire family? Can we *know* that displaying God's justice in the punishing of a rapist (either partially in this life, or even completely in a 'final judgment' to come) is more valuable than avoiding the rape altogether? Can we *know* that the good of societal cooperation to eradicate cancer outweighs… cancer? Can we *know* that my being awakened to spiritual things required my being cheated out of my life savings, and could not have occurred in any other way? Can we *know* that God's glory in justly punishing sinners could only come about through punishing genocidal maniacs and not, say, ordinary murderers? (A single person gets punished either way, right?) Isn't it clear that we *don't* know enough to make these kinds of judgments, in any particular case? We don't have an infinite number of theodicies, just four of them. And once we run through the list, that's it. So if we can't make our case that the good is both weighty and dependent, in any of the four contexts, what then? Well, I guess we stop trying, and give up.

Are the goods aimed at in the narratives about Job, Joseph, and Jesus both 'dependent goods' and 'weighty goods'? In the cases of Joseph and Jesus, these do indeed seem like weighty goods, for they involve nothing less than the provision of redemption itself, eternal deliverance from the consequences of sin. But are they dependent goods? Is the betrayal of Joseph the *only* way open to God to preserve his people from famine? Can't God just provide them food? In the case of Job's suffering, the good aimed at seems like a dependent good—you cannot get 'Job's great perseverance in the midst of great suffering' without great suffering—but is it really a weighty good? Is it clearly *better* to refute Satan's lies about Job by way of Job's suffering, than to simply leave Satan's lies unrefuted and spare Job the suffering? Why is putting Satan in his place so important, anyway?

Seen in this light, the time and space spent in this book on 'the way of theodicy' seems to be a colossal disaster. We are right back at the beginning, at the conclusion of chapter 1, and even worse off if that were possible, since it seems that the Christian now *knows* he is defenseless before the intellectual problem of evil. At least before, our former ignorance left us with some comfort, with the (still-living) hope that some clever religious believers somewhere had this problem sorted!

CAN THE CRITIC 'RULE OUT' THESE THEODICIES IN ANY PARTICULAR CASE?

And yet… what about that problem of evil in chapter 1? What was said about the burden of proof? It rests upon both parties, upon the critic and the Christian. And while the Christian's burden is to respond to the argument, the critic's burden is to *make* the argument. Some of the sharpest critics of theodicy, including the Greater-Good theodicy, are skeptics who press the problem of evil upon Christians. In pressing these points about our lack of knowledge in these areas of weightiness and dependence, I am pressing *their* points against Christian communities who dare to articulate theodicy. These skeptics are incredulous that such a flimsy project ever got developed and then sustained within the Christian church. There is sometimes even a tone of moral outrage, combined with the idea that attempts at theodicy add to rather than explain the evil in the world. In *The God Delusion*, biologist Richard Dawkins regards any attempt 'to justify suffering in a world run by God' as a 'grotesque piece of reasoning.'

In Psalm 76, the psalmist sings to God: 'Surely the wrath of man shall praise you; the remnant of wrath you will put on like a belt' (Ps. 76:10). And in this spirit, the sincere and passionate doubts of skeptics—that Christians can really pull off the theodicy project—can be both acknowledged and then turned around for the greater good, as something that helps Christians neutralize the problem of evil. If he who affirms must prove, then the question in the problem of evil is not whether Christians know enough to 'rule in' the applicability of a theodicy on any particular occasion, but whether critics know enough to 'rule out' the applicability of any theodicy.

The reason why the evils in the world are supposed to disprove God's existence is that such a God would have prevented them if he exists. But he would only have prevented them if he didn't have a good reason that justified him in permitting them. So the critic has to prove a universal negative: *there is no reason* that would justify God in permitting whatever difficult case of evil we are now choosing to think about. It is a claim about a certain territory—the reasons God could have for permitting evil—and a claim that that territory is *empty*.

At this point Christians need to be careful, lest they respond to the critic's claims in ways that are irrational and therefore unhelpful. For some of these significant cases of pain and suffering (let's admit it: for many!), it certainly *seems* as if God could have no good reason for permitting them, reasons which satisfy the weightiness and dependence standards. (An example discussed in the literature: a five-year-old raped and strangled by her mother's boyfriend.) A skeptic might tell a Christian, 'I'm sorry, but I've been thinking about this difficult case of evil for weeks now, and it just seems to me that there could be no justification for permitting it.' Christians shouldn't doubt the sincerity of these skeptics! Indeed, they shouldn't doubt what skeptics report as their *seemings*. Many Christians, similarly perplexed by the evil in the world, have the *same* seeming that the skeptic has! These Christians also scratch their heads and come up with nothing that satisfies the doubly austere constraints of theodicy.

In addition, Christians need to be careful not to deny that people (including skeptics) are quite rational in *appealing to* their seemings in order to come to justified conclusions about the world. It *seems* to me that I am typing at a keyboard right now. Isn't that as good a reason as any to think I *am* typing at a keyboard? It seems to me that it's my middle son's birthday today, as I check the calendar. (Why am I writing this book on such a day?!) Surely that's good reason to think *it is* his birthday.

Finally, Christians should be careful not to deny that people are often rational in drawing conclusions about the world based on their *negative* seemings. A 'negative seeming' occurs when it seems to me that something is *not* there. It seems to me that there isn't an elephant in my office. That's a great reason to think there is no such elephant. It doesn't *prove* there is no elephant, but it does make that denial highly likely to be true! So, to put the preceding three points together: *there's nothing irrational, at first glance, in the critic concluding something about a chosen territory based upon his negative seeming.* We do it with respect to elephants; why not with respect to God's reasons for suffering? In both cases, it just doesn't seem that the elephants or the justified reasons exist. Therefore, most likely, they don't exist. For many people, this means that the problem of evil is a good reason to reject God's existence after all.

However, the analogy to elephants is highly misleading. My perceptual capacities are such that elephants are discernible by me with the naked eye. Given my perceptual capacities, I would have seen an elephant if one were there. I don't see an elephant, so there isn't an elephant. Case closed. But we have excellent reason for thinking that things are relevantly different when it comes to discerning God's reasons for permitting particular cases of evil. *Are these the kinds of things we would discern by our cognitive capacities, if they were there?* Let's look at this from two angles, one philosophical and the other biblical.[3]

---

3   The philosophical reasoning should be of interest to skeptics, while the biblical reasoning will help confirm my point for Christians, and perhaps even convince skeptics that what can be known by philosophical argument on this point matches perfectly what can already be known by way of the Bible.

PHILOSOPHICAL ARGUMENT: SIX KINDS OF ANALOGY FOR OUR COGNITIVE LIMITATIONS

Perceptual analogies. It doesn't seem to me that there is a perfectly spherical rock right now on the dark side of the moon. Given obvious limits to my perceptual capacities, not to mention how I am currently situated with respect to the moon, even if such a spherical rock were there, I wouldn't have noticed. I *couldn't* have noticed! Maybe it's there, maybe it isn't. The point is that it doesn't follow from the fact that it *doesn't* seem to me as if the rock is there, that therefore it's likely—on the basis of this 'negative seeming'—that it's *not* there, that that particular lunar territory is *empty* of spherical rocks. For all I *know*, there *is* such a rock there, right now.

A more mundane example: I have a hundred trees in my backyard, and it doesn't seem to me that there are ladybugs crawling on any of them. I reflect on this fact very carefully as I look out of my bedroom window. I even struggle in vain for at least ten minutes to come up with principled arguments as to why they *would* be there. But it's no more likely after my reflections and intellectual struggles on this question than before, that there are no ladybugs on the trees. I can't tell one way or another, because they aren't the kinds of things perceivable by me at this distance.

Scientific analogies. The theories of special relativity (the physics of the very large and the very fast) and of quantum mechanics (the physics of the very small) are extremely complex but well-confirmed theories given current empirical data. But humans in earlier eras could hardly fathom these theories being *possibly* true, much less actually true! The inability of an early medieval scribe to invent, imagine, or comprehend such theories indicated nothing about whether the theories divulge important truths about the structure of the universe. Apparently, they do. Here it would be foolish to insist that the medievals *would* have discerned the truth of relativity if in fact it were a truth. History proves this suggestion false: they didn't.

Again, let's say I peruse a book on *Quantum Computing*, and—given my lack of expertise in quantum mechanics—it doesn't strike me as obvious that there's a necessary connection between what the author concludes at the end of chapter 1, and what he argues in chapter 2. To be honest, it all strikes me as gibberish. What follows from my failure to discern this connection? That there *isn't* one? That would be a tad premature, to say the least.

Moral analogies. How long did it take humans to discern that fundamental human rights of one sort or another were in fact *fundamental* human rights, despite the fact that millennia of previous humans missed this? Given that, is it not reasonable to suppose that there are other goods to be aimed at which we do not presently discern? Don't we nowadays recognize a necessary connection between humans being the kind of beings they are, and various kinds of human rights they all enjoy regardless of sex, race, or class? (Well, most of us do, and hopefully you the reader do.) But for the vast majority of human history, we didn't even discern these universal moral truths as *being* truths.

Linguistic analogies. Let's say I am a quantum physicist, but I don't know a lick of Greek. I hear my colleague down the hall reading Plato's *Apology* to his class, in the original language. It surely seems to me that the sentences I am hearing have no meaning. (For a moment, I even confuse what I am hearing with the harsh speech of Klingons, and think the professor is yet again showing *Star Trek* episodes to his class. What do I know?) It doesn't follow from any of this, from its seeming to me that the spoken sentences have no meaning, that it's likely the spoken sentences have no meaning.

Aesthetic analogies. True story: I'm listening to Beethoven's *Ninth Symphony* in my music class at UCLA. I'm quite pleased by the melodies. But I utterly fail to grasp that this symphony (like his *Fifth*) illustrates one of Beethoven's most crucial contributions to the development of symphonic form. Whereas in Mozart's day the 'sonata form' (exposition of theme, then its development, then its recapitulation) were the elements in order of each individual movement of a symphony, Beethoven projected this form onto the symphony as a whole, so that the earlier movements are exposition and development, and then the last movement is recapitulation. This gives the entire musical work a fundamental unity it would not otherwise have had. I am even told that the *Ninth Symphony* in particular illustrates the quest for the perfect musical instrument, which is finally found at the end (the human voice). I am utterly oblivious to musical values like this. Having little musical training, I could probably listen to the symphony a hundred times and never notice these facts. It doesn't follow from my ignorance that Beethoven *didn't* have this purpose, much less that he was unsuccessful in executing it.

Parental analogies. Another true story: my firstborn son has to get his 'jabs' while we are in Oxford. As a nurse explains, he must be removed from the presence of his parents to receive these inoculations (the idea is that the child would suffer *more* being subjected to this pain in the presence of parents who are sitting there doing nothing, than being subjected to it in their absence). While the pain is brief, we do hear him crying in the next room while getting the shots. Let's say it appears to him quite strongly that there is simply no good reason for his experiencing this pain. It doesn't follow that there is no good reason. As a one-year-old, it isn't likely that he would come up with the reason, even if there was one (and there is!).

Application: discerning the weightiness or dependence of goods. What do these analogies have in common (beyond the fact that some of them were inspired by things written by Christian philosophers Stephen Wykstra and William Alston)? They each emphasize our cognitive limitations with respect to discerning goods and connections in territories where we lack the relevant expertise. Once we recognize these limitations, we should also see that certain inferences we are tempted to make about such territories are positively irrational. The Enlightenment skeptic David Hume, quoted in chapter 1 as a source of the problem of evil, anticipates the point I am making here. After stating the problem, he exclaims in triumph: 'Nothing can shake the solidity of this reasoning, so short, so clear, so decisive….' But he immediately acknowledges a way out of the reasoning: '… except we assert that these subjects exceed all human capacity, and that our common measures of truth and falsehood are not applicable to them.'

God is omniscient, which means he not only knows everything that *we* are likely to guess at, but every truth whatsoever. This is an extraordinary degree of knowledge, and it means that God knows things that we cannot at present even fathom. As the above analogies suggest, this is easily demonstrated for a huge range of cases. If the complexities of an infinite God's divine plan for the unfolding of the universe *does* involve God's recognizing either deep goods, or necessary connections between various evils and the realization of those goods, or both of these things, would our inability to discern these goods or connections give us a reason for thinking they aren't there? What would be the basis of such confidence? But without such confidence, we have little reason to accept premise 2 of the problem of evil. So we have little reason to accept its conclusion.

Beyond this, what about individual cases of pain and suffering? Do we *really* know enough to rule out punishment, soul-building, megaphone, or higher-order goods, in these particular cases, as being the goods both aimed at and only obtainable by these means? Why couldn't God be punishing someone for his sins? Isn't he allowed to do that without our permission? What do we *know* that rules this out? Why couldn't someone's character be defective in a way we can't perceive—perhaps their selfishness is known only to them and God—such that these circumstances are perfectly suited above all others to help them improve? As theologian Sinclair Ferguson puts it, the spiritual growth of persons is like an iceberg: at least ninety percent is 'below sea level,' outside the awareness of the people around them. Using outer appearances as a guide to what's going on beneath the surface is a woefully unreliable indicator of people's needs, struggles, victories, and failures. I said earlier that we seem to have ample reason for thinking that soul-building *doesn't* occur in many cases of suffering. But do we really know this? And why couldn't someone be so addicted to the vanities of the world, that they need this pain as God's megaphone? If the method of God's causality is hidden from us (previous chapter), why not the content of his purposes (this chapter)? (As Christian philosopher Alvin Plantinga suggests, maybe it's simply the case that God's reason is just too complicated for us to understand. Do we know that's *not* the case?)

BIBLICAL ARGUMENT: PASSAGES THAT ENCOURAGE RECOGNIZING OUR COGNITIVE LIMITATIONS

The theme of divine inscrutability is not only exceedingly defensible common sense. It also looms large in the Bible, having both pastoral and apologetic implications. It closes both the mouths of Christians who would insensitively offer 'God's reasons' to those who suffer (when they don't know such reasons) and the mouths of critics who would irrationally preclude there being divine reasons for the suffering. Imagine we were on the scene in the cases of Job (as his friend), Joseph (as his brother), and Jesus (as his tormentor). Would we have been able to guess at God's purpose for the suffering? Would we not instead have been wholly unaware of any such purpose? Does not a large part of the literary power of the Bible's narrative, and the spiritual encouragement it offers, rest upon this interplay between the ignorance of the human actors and the wisdom of divine providence?

Job's case is particularly instructive, for his situation is clearly *our* situation. We are of course *unlike* Job, for we have access to the prologue of chapters 1 and 2, whereas Job did not. Even when God leaves Job at the end of the book without a clue as to divine purposes in his life—preferring instead to reinforce to Job his abysmal ignorance of how God brought about and orders the natural world—we are given the insight not afforded to Job. But that's only because we, unlike Job, have the special, verbal revelation from God that constitutes chapters 1 and 2. When we put down the book of Job, and reflect upon our own suffering and the suffering of those around us, we may wish for a similar prologue to our life's story, something that will inform and illuminate our particular experiences of suffering. But apart from the very *general* ideas enshrined in the four theodicies of this chapter, and promises like that of Romans 8:28, we are left wholly in the dark as to the particulars. Job is an everyman. In being privileged to see *his* prologue we are not like him, but in remaining ignorant of *our own* prologue we are just like him. The book of Job may assure us that *there is* an illuminating prologue for our lives, involving a divine pursuit of weighty, dependent goods. But it doesn't give it to us. There may not be room in all the books of the world to write these out for every human life, much less room in the Bible. And even as Job's ignorance rightly prevents him from credibly launching accusations against God, so our ignorance of God's plans and purposes should lead us to cover our mouths as well.

As we've seen, people regularly misapply the punishment theodicy in the Bible: Job's friends ('Confess your sin, Job!'), Jesus's disciples ('Why did the tower fall?' 'Why Pilate's bloodshed?' 'Why was the man born blind?'), Maltese natives ('The god Justice sent that poisonous snake…')— all go wrong in attributing suffering to punishment in particular cases. Only a fool would think he could do better in his guesswork. The way of theodicy is the way of the fool, if you insist on ruling it in *or* ruling it out, and the way of the wise is to know this.

In the end, God calls his people to recognize that they would *never* be able to guess at God's reasons for various evils. Faced with the apostasy of his Jewish kinsmen who rejected Jesus, Paul was confident in chapters 9 through 11 of the book of Romans that God had a plan here, even for these evils, and he explains that plan in those chapters. But he only knew that plan by God's revelation. When he learned that 'God has consigned all to disobedience, that he may have mercy on all' (Rom. 11:32), it led Paul to cry out:

> Oh, the depth of the riches and wisdom and knowledge of God! How unsearchable are his judgments and how inscrutable his ways! 'For who has known the mind of the Lord, or who has been his counselor?' 'Or who has given a gift to him that he might be repaid?' For from him and through him and to him are all things. To him be glory forever. Amen. (Rom. 11:33–36)

Here the themes of divine sovereignty over evil ('from him… are all things') and divine inscrutability in the midst of evil ('how inscrutable his ways!') are blended together in a paean of humble praise. As the seventeenth-century English Puritan Thomas Watson put it: 'Faith knows there are no impossibilities with God, and will trust him where it cannot trace him.' To the extent that God has not spoken about a particular event in history, his judgments *are* unsearchable, and his paths *are* beyond tracing out. But that does not mean there is not a greater good which justifies God's purposing of that event.

CONCLUSION

No doubt some objections have been raised in readers' minds while considering this chapter. Isn't playing the inscrutability card a 'cop out' of Christian responsibility when it comes to defending the faith? Doesn't this approach lead to a general skepticism about all moral knowledge whatsoever? If 'for all we know' evils lead to a greater good, why can't it be that 'for all we know' these same evils will lead to a *worse* evil instead? And why have I completely left out of my presentation two kinds of theodicy that have proved popular among my fellow Christians: appeal to free will (to explain moral evil), and appeal to the laws of nature (to explain natural evil)?

These are good questions. I will defer answering most of them until the last chapter, which surveys quite a few objections to the argument of the entire book. But we'll look at this very last question, in the next chapter.

SUMMARY OF MAIN POINTS

- There are four kinds of Greater-Good theodicy: punishment (God displaying his justice), soul-building (God displaying his goodness), pain-as-God's-megaphone (God displaying his mercy), and higher-order goods (God aiming at goods that are good precisely because they respond to and overcome the evils of the world).

- Christians do not know enough to 'rule in' one of these four theodicies as applying to any particular case of evil.

- But *critics* do not know enough to 'rule out' any of these four theodicies as applying to any particular case of evil.

- Six kinds of analogy argue for our cognitive limitations in discerning divine reasons for permitting suffering: perceptual, scientific, moral, linguistic, aesthetic, and parental.

- There are many passages in the Bible that similarly encourage recognizing our cognitive limitations in this respect.

5

Can Free Will or the Laws of Nature Solve the Problem of Evil?

In the previous chapter I sketched out four theodicies—punishment, soul-building, pain-as-God's-megaphone, and higher-order goods—and argued that 'the way of the wise' is to accept that we don't know enough to 'rule in' *or* 'rule out' any of these theodicies as applying to any instance of moral or natural evil. The fact that we don't know enough to *rule them in* means that Christians should shut their mouths rather than confidently declare 'God's reason' for the evils they see. But the fact that we don't know enough to *rule them out* means that skeptics are without a reason for accepting premise 2 of the problem of evil. They have no reason for accepting the idea that 'A perfectly good being *will* prevent evil as far as he can.' For if the theodicy *does* apply to an instance of evil (and we don't know enough to rule this out!), then in these instances a perfectly good being *does* have a good reason for not preventing an evil he could prevent. My argument in chapters 2 through 4 has been that licensing and limiting the Greater-Good theodicy in this way provides a reasonable response to the problem of evil.

But why stop at just these four theodicies? As I said in the Preface, what about all the *other* things Christians have said in response to the problem of evil? Could either 'free will' or 'the laws of nature' be appealed to as worthwhile theodicies? There are supposed to be two great advantages of these two theodicies. First, they don't involve in any way God's *intending* that evils come to pass, much less the idea that the evils are *required means* to any goods that God intends to come to pass. Rather, the evils of the world are the *unintended* by-product of God's aiming to provide us two great goods: the good of free choice, and the good of having a stable environment in which to exercise that free choice. If God is going to provide us with those goods initially, and if he is going to maintain those goods over time, then both he and we will be stuck with the *moral evils* that occur when we abuse free will, and with the *natural evils* that occur when a stable environment makes things painful for us. God can't give us free will without the possibility that we'll abuse it, and God can't give us a stable environment without the possibility that it causes us pain. And that leads us to the second great advantage: combining the free will and stable environment theodicies gives us a neat way of explaining *all* evils whatsoever, whether moral or natural. Moral evils become possible when there's free will, and natural evils become possible when there's a stable environment. And this is exactly what many Christians have argued.[1]

My reason for not incorporating these two theodicies into my overall response to the problem of evil is that these appearances are deceiving. The theodicies don't have the two advantages commonly advertised. First, they are inadequate in and of themselves, for they don't provide a satisfactory reason for God to permit moral evil or natural evil. Second, they are irrelevant in providing a genuine contrast with the theodicies I've already appealed to, for they don't avoid the key idea that is implicit in those other theodicies: that God intends that evils come to pass for a greater good. And because they are inadequate and irrelevant, I don't think it's wise to appeal to them as a way of neutralizing the problem of evil. I'll support both points as I discuss these theodicies in the rest of this chapter.

---

1   For example, one finds the free-will theodicy in the early church father Augustine and in many other writers, and one finds the stable environment theodicy in the twentieth-century Christian writer C. S. Lewis.

THE FREE-WILL THEODICY: MORAL EVIL IS DUE TO HUMAN ABUSE OF FREE WILL

The free-will theodicy stated. The free-will theodicy depends on accepting two key ideas: the value of free will, and the unfortunate consequences of there being free will. Put these two ideas together, and you have a good reason for God to permit moral evil. The first idea is a kind of value judgment that any world *with* free will (no matter how that free will may be abused) will be *more valuable* than a world *without* free will. So, for instance, God could have created a 'desert world,' a world with mountains and trees and rivers and deserts, but with no humans (or any other creatures with free will). That world would certainly have great value, and would testify to the goodness, wisdom, power, and glory of its Creator. But it would have something missing: the gift of free will. And in missing that, it would be missing one of the things that we most deeply value: the ability to *freely* enter relationships of love with our fellow humans and with God, the ability to *freely* decide to take responsibility for one another's welfare, and the ability to *freely* cooperate with one another in communal projects of great significance (such as the pursuit of scientific discovery, cultural production, and historical inquiry). Indeed, perhaps in having free will we most resemble our Creator (the most valuable being of all), who freely created all things and freely sustains them over time to realize great purposes of his own. These things would all be missing in a world without free will. Likewise for a 'robot world' in which there are creatures very much like us, but whose every action is determined ahead of time. The 'love,' 'decision-making,' 'responsibility,' and 'cooperation' in such a world (it is alleged) wouldn't be the real thing but a pale, mocking imitation of it. No, a free-willed world will always be more valuable than a desert world or a robot world.

But if God is going to give us this extraordinarily valuable gift of free will, and therefore the sole means for enjoying all the goods just named, then we need to acknowledge the unfortunate consequences of there being such a powerful gift: free will gives its possessors the ability to do evil as well as good. God can't give us a choice *between* good and evil, and then preclude our exercising that ability as we wish. Such divine intervention would be tantamount to taking back the gift once given. So God must permit our abuses of free will—that is, moral evil—for such permission is the price he must pay to get us free will in the first place. But free will is so valuable that this trade-off is worth it. A world with free will and much moral good, but with lots of moral evil, is still going to be far more valuable than worlds without free will or moral good altogether. Free will then satisfies both constraints on theodicy that we accepted in chapter 2, for it is a weighty and dependent good. It's weighty, for it's one of the most valuable gifts we could ever receive. It's dependent, because its actual exercise depends on our having at least the *possibility* to use it in very bad ways. For God to remove that possibility would be to remove the gift itself, and therefore its value.

The inadequacy of the free-will theodicy. Despite all this, prospects are dim for the gift of free will being able to bear the explanatory weight this theodicy puts upon it. Advocates of this theodicy are right to think that if we really have this freedom to choose between good and evil, then not even God can *give* us the possibility of choosing either good or evil, and yet *remove* the possibility of choosing either good or evil. That seems contradictory, and God can't be blamed for failing to do the contradictory. But of greater concern is the value judgment itself: *is* free will as valuable as claimed, such that any world with it is automatically more valuable than any world without it? That seems quite suspect, for at least three reasons.

First, consider a situation of *restricted free will*. As Michael Murray puts it (summarizing an argument from philosopher Peter Geach): 'God could have simply given us free choice among only good alternatives… it is surely plausible that *God could have wired us so that thoughts of evil acts never occurred to us*, while thoughts of diverse good courses of action always would, thus leaving us plenty of genuine alternatives in choice' (my emphasis). This is not a situation in which God is always intervening, blocking our free choices from having their ordinary consequences. (That would remove significant free will altogether.) It is instead a situation in which God restricts *the range of thoughts* that could occur to us in the first place. Thoughts of bad actions wouldn't occur to us. In such a situation, we would still be the ultimate causes of our choices. And for any good thing we choose to do (meditate on God, study science, pursue a friendship, walk the dog, bake a cake) we could have refrained from choosing that, and chosen to do something else instead. So this is not a world in which we are ever *determined* to choose the things we choose. It's neither a 'desert world' nor a 'robot world.' *But it would be a world without moral evil.* So why would the world that the free-will theodicist insists on—a world with *unrestricted* free will, the ability to do good and evil—be *more* valuable than this kind of world? Yes, a world with 'limited free will' has something missing from it: human beings actually thinking evil thoughts and doing evil things! But is *that* something God would find to be so valuable that for its sake he would permit all the horrific evils we find all around us? That seems most implausible. Why would the value of free will consist specifically in the opportunity it gives us *to do moral evil*? What's so valuable about *that*? So given this possibility of restricted free will, the value judgment about unrestricted free will just looks false. But that's the value judgment that needs to be true if the free-will theodicy is to succeed.

Second, consider the situation of *God's free will*. The Bible teaches that 'God cannot be tempted with evil' (James 1:13). After all, if God is perfectly knowledgeable he would always know what is the morally right thing to do, and if God is all-powerful, then he would not be subject to any outside forces that could keep him from doing the morally right thing. But if he cannot even be *tempted* with evil, then certainly he cannot do evil, that is, make evil choices. In the traditional theological terminology, God is 'impeccable' or 'necessarily good'. That is part of his greatness, that he is impervious to the kind of corruption and moral weakness that so often afflicts us. But God is supposed to be the most valuable being it is possible for there to be. And if free will is so valuable, as valuable as free-will theodicists say, is it not counter-intuitive to think that we puny humans have a great-making property that God lacks? What makes for a *really valuable* kind of existence, says the advocate of the free-will theodicy, is the possession of unrestricted free will, the ability to do evil as well as good. *But then it turns out that the most valuable being in the universe doesn't have this kind of freedom.* Does God just have a 'pale, mocking imitation' of 'love,' 'decision-making,' 'responsibility,' and 'cooperation,' instead of the real thing? That seems hard to accept. Viewed from this perspective, the value judgment at the heart of the free-will theodicy seems contradicted by the nature of the Being it seeks to defend.

Third, consider the situation of *heavenly free will*. It is a common understanding of heaven that its inhabitants cannot choose evil. The 'heavenly Jerusalem', that is, 'the assembly of the firstborn who are enrolled in heaven', is the abode of 'the spirits of the righteous made perfect' (Heb.12:22–23). These perfected people will be sinners no more, for their Savior 'is able to keep you from stumbling and to present you blameless before the presence of his glory with great joy' (Jude 1:24). In heaven, the three great sources of temptation—the world, the flesh, and the devil—will be gone, and so there will be no opportunity for sinning, because no opportunity for temptation to sin. If this is correct, then heaven is a place where we *lack* a kind of freedom: the freedom to do evil. (In this respect it will be a place similar to the 'restricted free-will' scenario we earlier considered, except that this place is *actual* and not merely possible.) But heaven is supposed to be the most valuable place it is possible for there to be. And if free will is so valuable, as valuable as free-will theodicists say, is it not counter-intuitive to think that our earthly life has a great-making property that heaven lacks? What makes for a *really valuable* kind of existence, says the advocate of the free-will theodicy, is the possession of unrestricted free will, the ability to do evil as well as good. *But then it turns out that the most valuable place in the universe doesn't have this kind of freedom.* Do the saints in heaven, throughout all eternity, just have a 'pale, mocking imitation' of 'love,' 'decision-making,' 'responsibility,' and 'cooperation,' instead of the real thing? That seems hard to accept. Viewed from this perspective, the value judgment at the heart of the free-will theodicy seems contradicted by the value of the most valuable kind of life possible: worship and eternal happiness in the presence of God himself.

THE NATURAL LAW THEODICY: NATURAL EVIL IS DUE TO THE LAWS OF NATURE

The natural law theodicy stated. So much for the free-will theodicy. What about the natural law theodicy? The natural law (or 'stable environment') theodicy depends on accepting two key ideas: the need for laws of nature and the unfortunate consequences of there being laws of nature. Put these two ideas together, and you have a good reason for God to permit natural evil. The first idea asserts that if there is going to be meaningful choice-making of any kind, then we need to have reliable expectations of the immediate consequences of our choices. If we open a door, it can't be that doors (when opened) may randomly turn into poison gas that kills us. If we pick up our toothbrush, it can't be that toothbrushes (when picked up) may randomly turn into ferocious tigers that eat us. If that's what the world is like, then we'll end up curled into a fetal position in the corner of the room all day, afraid to make *any* choices, for a chaotic world with no regularities is a world in which choice-making is extremely foolish, dangerous, and most likely impossible. Only with the confidence that there are in fact 'laws of nature' can we make intelligible choices and realize our intentions and goals in a stable environment.

But if God is going to give us this stable environment in which to live, an environment governed by laws of nature with respect to gravity, inertia, aerodynamics, plate tectonics, and oxygenation, then we need to acknowledge the unfortunate consequences of there being such a stable environment: laws of nature can produce pain and suffering when we 'bump up against' their hardness and inflexibility. If their 'stability' depended upon the whims and choices of individual human beings, being alternately enforced and suspended at will, then they couldn't be relied upon by human beings in general. God won't suspend these laws simply because their operation might on occasion prove inconvenient to us, as that would undermine the stability of the environment they provide. If we decide to dance on the edge of a cliff, and then stumble, God is not going to temporarily repeal the law of gravity so that we float to the ground like a feather. If we foolishly leave our hand in the path of a closing car door, God won't suddenly suspend laws about the inertia of large metal objects. The same law of conservation of momentum that enables you to shake someone's hand without punching him is the same law that guarantees you'll be crushed by a boulder speeding toward you if you don't jump out of the way. Thus, there can be pain—quite a bit of pain!—when we live in an environment governed by these kinds of regularities. That's the price you pay when you live in a stable environment that enables you to engage in meaningful choice-making. You can't benefit from that aspect of the laws and then wish there were no such laws!

The inadequacy of the natural law theodicy. So the natural law theodicy lays it down as a dictum: a stable environment requires the possibility of natural evil. Allegedly, God can't get one without the other, and so natural evil is the price God pays to get us stability (and therefore the possibility of meaningful choice-making). But in contradiction to this, the Bible teaches that there *are* two environments that God has provided or will provide that are perfectly stable but are free from natural evil. These are the Garden of Eden (before human beings rebelled against God), and heaven (after human beings are restored to perfect fellowship with God). If this is true, then the principle upon which the natural law theodicy relies is simply false.

What if Adam hadn't sinned? What if he and Eve had continued in perfect fellowship with God? Are we really to imagine that an innocent Adam and Eve would have been subject to all sorts of natural evil for the rest of their (immortal) lives? And what about heaven? Isn't this a place without natural evil—without pain and without suffering? Isn't this a place in which 'he will wipe away every tear from their eyes, and death shall be no more, neither shall there be mourning, nor crying, nor pain anymore, for the former things have passed away' (Rev. 21:4)? Won't he be 'making all things new' (Rev. 21:5), so that 'no longer will there be anything accursed' (Rev. 22:3)?

But the Garden of Eden and heaven are surely places in which there is a lot of intelligent choice-making. Humans were to 'work and keep' the garden (Gen. 2:15), and to seek to exercise responsible dominion and stewardship over the earth as God had commanded (Gen. 1:26, 28). That would involve quite a bit of decision-making on their part over longer periods of time. In 'the new heavens and the new earth' (Rev. 21:1), there will be unhindered fellowship between God and humans, and among humans themselves. There will be social community and cultural production (Rev. 21:24–26). Surely this also will involve numerous decisions day-by-day, throughout all eternity, on the part of its inhabitants. So the characteristic claim of the 'stable environment' theodicy, that stable environments *require* the possibility of natural evil, seems to be contradicted by two of the most important environments described in the Bible.

THE IRRELEVANCE OF THESE THEODICIES

Distinguishing 'general' Greater-Good theodicy from 'particular' Greater-Good theodicy. I said earlier that the free-will and natural law theodicies were supposed to have two great advantages over the four theodicies I endorsed in the last chapter. We've now seen that the first great advantage simply doesn't pan out. Free will and laws of nature *don't* give us a neat way of explaining *all* evils whatsoever, whether moral or natural, because the explanations proposed don't work. At the very least, they seem to conflict with other, important things that Christians want to say on the basis of the Bible. They are inadequate to the purpose.

But there is supposed to be a second great advantage of these theodicies: they don't involve God's *intending* that any evils come to pass. Rather, moral and natural evil is always the divinely *unintended* by-product of God's aiming to provide us with something else: the great goods of free choice and a stable environment in which to exercise that free choice. The idea is that God's goodness will be more apparent to us if we are assured that God *doesn't* intend that any evils come to pass. On these theodicies, he certainly doesn't *decide* that they will come to pass; he's just stuck with them because they became a possibility when he decided to seek *other* things in our lives.

One way we can see this (alleged) contrast is to introduce two labels: *'general' Greater-Good theodicy* and *'particular' Greater-Good theodicy*. In each kind of theodicy, God is pursuing great goods in the midst of allowing various evils. But in 'general' Greater-Good theodicy, God creates a structured universe that operates according to general principles (free-willed creatures in a stable environment governed by laws of nature), because only in such an environment can the goods come to pass. In so doing God is pursuing *general* policies that allow moral and natural evils in his universe. But he intends *none* of the particular evils that occur.

The free-will and natural law theodicies are supposed to be examples of this. In the free-will theodicy, God adopts a general policy toward his creation: 'Let there be free will, but I won't plan particular acts of free will.' So if we abuse our free will and cause pain and suffering in each other's lives, God didn't plan for that to come to pass. And in the natural law theodicy, God adopts yet another general policy toward his creation: 'Let there be laws of nature, but I won't plan for these laws to produce pain in any particular instance.' So if we suffer pain due to the laws of nature, God didn't plan for that to come to pass either. Rather, what God planned for is the 'greater good' of the very existence of the creation order, with free-willed creatures making choices in a relatively stable environment. Any evils that arise in such an environment, whether moral or natural, are never intended by God. Rather, it is the *value* of such an environment, and the *value* of the goods that could arise in such an environment, which God intends.

In effect, *'general' Greater-Good theodicy* is a building with a foundation of free will and a scaffolding of natural laws. Moral goods and evils, and natural goods and evils, arise within this building and can arise nowhere else. But moral and natural evils are in the world due to *general* policies God pursues, rather than because of *particular* choices he has made which ensure their occurrence. In this way we can explain both kinds of evil without attributing to God any intention that any particular evils come to pass. *God only intends the goods and never intends the evils,* for the evils don't *have* to occur in order for the goods to occur. In fact, God hopes the goods will occur without the evils! God's general policies *may* give rise to unintended evils (both moral and natural), but their unintended reality is the price God must sometimes pay to get the goods.

By way of contrast, *'particular' Greater-Good theodicy* is supposed to be very different from this. On this view, God doesn't merely pursue 'general policies' toward his creation, while refraining from making any decisions that ensure that particular evils come to pass. Rather, as surprising as it sounds, God *does* ensure that particular evils come to pass, because he knows these evils *are* the necessary means of bringing about particular, greater goods. In the punishment, soul-building, pain-as-God's-megaphone, and higher-order goods theodicies discussed in the last chapter, God intends that particular evils come to pass as a means of bringing about these goods in particular cases. So if Christians think it is important that God have nothing to do with 'intending' and 'ensuring' that significant cases of pain and suffering come to pass, it is 'general' and not 'particular' Greater-Good theodicy that they must offer. Or so it seems.

The reduction of 'general' Greater-Good theodicy to 'particular' Greater-Good theodicy. Again, though, appearances are deceiving. As a matter of fact, the free-will and natural law theodicies aren't really an *alternative* to the four theodicies I endorsed earlier, with respect to divine intent. It turns out that when you think a bit harder about 'general' Greater-Good theodicy, it all reduces to 'particular' Greater-Good theodicy anyway. And so the advertised contrast dissolves. Here's why.

The Bible says that God has *often* miraculously intervened in the creation order he has set up. For instance, he has directly intervened in order to prevent *moral* evil, by either suspending or ending altogether a creature's exercise of free will. When two priests named Nadab and Abihu (sons of Aaron the high priest in the Old Testament) violated God's express command and offered up unauthorized sacrifices to God in the tabernacle, contrary to God's command,

God prevented their further disobedience by striking them down in spectacular fashion. 'Fire came out from before the LORD and consumed them, and they died before the LORD' (Lev. 10:2). So God ended Nadab's and Abihu's freely chosen but rebellious mode of worship, rather than allowing it to continue. God didn't have to do this. He could have refrained from intervening, and allowed it to continue instead. But he decided to intervene, thus ending Nadab's and Abihu's abuse of free will and precluding any further moral evil on their part.

In addition, God has often directly intervened in order to prevent *natural* evil, by performing some miracle of nature and thereby suspending a law of nature. When the divided Red Sea threatened to drown the Israelites as they passed through to the other side, God miraculously kept the waters in place (cf. Exod. 14:21–22), thus preventing the natural evil of drowning that would have otherwise occurred. When the storm on the Sea of Galilee threatened to drown the disciples in their little boat, Jesus rebuked the wind and calmed the sea, thereby preventing the natural evil of drowning that would have otherwise occurred. Again, God didn't have to do either of these things. In each case he could have refrained from miraculously intervening, thus allowing the natural evil of drowning. But he decided to intervene, temporarily suspending a law of nature in order to preclude a case of natural evil (cf. Matt. 8:23–27; Mark 4:35–41).

Examples like these could be multiplied. God decides to keep pagan king Abimelech from sinning against him, in the matter of violating Abraham's wife Sarah (Gen. 20:6). God miraculously sends a great fish to swallow the prophet Jonah and keep him from drowning (Jonah 1:17). In response to the wickedness of mankind, God sent a highly destructive flood that eliminated innumerable humans from the earth, precluding them from making free-will choices at all (Gen. 6–7). In response to the moral evil of Egyptian slavery, God miraculously intervened and ended that institution of oppression against his people, going so far as to curse crops, livestock, and water supply, kill the firstborn among the Egyptians, and drown their army (Exod. 7–14). God miraculously struck down a Herod who blasphemously received worship from others, so that he breathed his last in the very midst of his sin (Acts 12:20–23). In both Old Testament and New Testament, God miraculously heals many people from naturally occurring diseases that they would otherwise have continued to suffer. And so on with respect to a great many miracles in the Bible. In these and many other cases, God overrode both human free will and the stability of the laws of nature in order to *eliminate* these particular evils. That is, he judged that his general policies of upholding free will and a stable environment *would not be undermined* by divine intervention in these cases. These are all decisions God made, and now here is the point: it would be extremely odd to think that divine *interventions* such as these require decisions on God's part, but divine *permission* does not.

So, take any instance in which God *permits* a case of moral evil or natural evil. This *also* involves a decision on God's part. If we assume the free-will and natural law theodicies, then when God *permits* evil in a particular case, it's because he judges that the good effects of permission *outweigh* the bad effects of intervention. That is, continuing to uphold free will and a stable environment *in this case* is more important to God than eliminating the evil. That's surely God's call to make, in each and every case of divine permission of evil, but one can't pretend that it doesn't involve a particular *decision* on God's part. Likewise, take any instance in which God prevents a case of moral evil or natural evil. This will obviously also involve a decision on God's part: he judges that the good effects of intervening *outweigh* the bad effects of permission. That is, eliminating the evil *in this case* is more important to God than continuing to uphold free will and a stable environment. And that again is surely God's call to make, in each and every case of divine preventing of evil, and it will involve a particular *decision* on God's part.

It follows that, even if we assume the free-will and natural law theodicies, *each and every case of moral evil and natural evil is due to a decision on God's part that that case of evil should exist.* For if he hadn't decided to permit it, he would have prevented it. And it was open to him to prevent it. And so 'general' Greater-Good theodicy collapses into 'particular' Greater-Good theodicy. The contrast between the two categories is lost, and we are left with the view that God makes particular decisions that ensure that particular, significant cases of pain and suffering come to pass. This is not what the traditional advocates of these two theodicies would have us believe, but it does seem to be a consequence of the theodicies once we take seriously the Bible's teaching about God's prerogative to prevent or permit particular evils. Even his permissions are *willing* permissions, done for particular reasons. It follows that even on these theodicies, God's choices ensure whether or not any *particular* case of moral or natural evil will exist. For if he allows it, he allows it for the greater good of upholding his general policy in *that* instance. And if he prevents it, he prevents it for the greater good of having a universe in which that evil doesn't exist. As long as God doesn't uphold his policies in *all* instances, then the relevance of these kinds of divine choices must be acknowledged. Thus, the ultimate reason why individual moral and natural evils occur is because of God's individual decisions that they occur.

In fact, the Bible never hints that the preceding theodicies are God's reasons for evils. Perhaps it is just as well that the two great advantages claimed for the free-will and natural law theodicies aren't advantages after all. For as a matter of fact, the Bible never hints that these two theodicies are ever God's reasons for permitting evils! The Bible never says that he allows moral evil for the sake of free will, or that he allows natural evil for the sake of a stable environment. Strictly speaking, this doesn't mean that the theodicies must be *false*. But in this respect they are to be contrasted with the four theodicies mentioned in the previous chapter, each of which has ample biblical support (punishment, soul-building, pain-as-God's-megaphone, higher-order goods).

In addition, there are plenty of occasions in the Bible where one would *expect* the author to mention the free-will or natural law theodicies, if in fact they are God's reasons for permitting evils. For example, in Romans 9 the apostle Paul is trying to explain to his readers why so many Israelites have failed to believe in Jesus as the Messiah. Has God rejected his people? One would expect that Paul would explain their evil of rejecting God's Son in light of their abuse of free will. But this is precisely what he does not do, preferring instead to trace their rejection back to the sovereign will and purpose of God (Rom. 9:14–24). Or consider natural disasters, such as famine, drought, rampaging wild animals, disease, birth defects, and disastrous weather. The Bible never traces these back to unfortunate and unintended side-effects of stable laws of nature. As we saw in chapter 3, these are again traced back to the sovereign purpose of God. Indeed, the idea that all moral and natural evils are *unintended* by God is contrary to what we saw in chapter 2, when we considered the cases of Job, Joseph, and Jesus. The Bible repeatedly refers to the divine intention behind the kinds of evils they experienced, as he aims at great goods by way of them.

For all these reasons, it seems unwise for Christians to espouse theodicies that aren't found in the Bible (and which the Bible seems to contradict), instead of theodicies that seem to be explicitly encouraged in the Bible. As noted in the Preface, it would be foolish for Christians to hide the teachings of the Bible from those who are skeptical about the truth of the Christian faith, in order to ultimately persuade them to embrace the teachings of the Bible.

SUMMARY OF MAIN POINTS

- The free-will theodicy says that moral evil is due to human abuse of free will, whereas the natural law theodicy says that natural evil is due to the laws of nature.

- Put together, the theodicies claim that the evils of the world are the unintended by-product of God's aiming to provide us with two great goods: the good of free choice, and the good of having a stable environment in which to exercise that free choice.

- Both theodicies are supposed to avoid the view that God intends that evils come to pass as the required means for goods that he also intends to come to pass.

- The free-will theodicy is subject to the problems of restricted free will, God's lack of free will, and heavenly lack of free will.

- The natural law theodicy is subject to the problems of choice-making in the Garden of Eden, and choice-making in heaven.

- Neither theodicy avoids the view that God intends and even ensures that evils come to pass for a greater good.

- Unlike the four theodicies presented in the previous chapter, the Bible never hints that the free-will and natural law theodicies are God's reasons for permitting evils.

6

Objections

INTRODUCTION

This book has taken a particular stance on God's relation to the evils in the world. While God is not a sinner who commits any sins, he is the sovereign creator and providential sustainer of the world, who ensures that natural and moral evils come to pass as necessary means for bringing about great goods that outweigh the evils. I have argued at length that this is a view that the Bible positively teaches, and that prospects are dim for the skeptic of the Christian faith being able to successfully argue that things are *not* this way.

Still, taking such a bold and definite position is bound to generate controversy among Christian and skeptic alike. It may have struck many readers that, even if decent arguments have been given for my position, my overall point of view is asking them to pay far too high a price. There are just too many *obvious* objections to looking at things in this way. This chapter is an attempt to consider and turn back the more popular criticisms that have been made to the approach I've advocated.

Many criticisms object to the structure of the theodicy itself: a 'Greater-Good' theodicy as outlined in chapter 2. Other criticisms point out alleged negative consequences of endorsing a 'high' view of divine sovereignty in chapter 3, by which the theodicy was licensed. Still other criticisms point out alleged negative consequences of appealing to divine inscrutability in chapter 4, by which the theodicy was limited. Some objections are more theoretical, while others focus on alleged practical difficulties that the theodicy poses for everyday life.

A common thread running through many of my replies in this chapter is that we must take the doctrines of divine sovereignty and inscrutability *together*. The former is about how reality is, whereas the latter is about our limited perspective on how reality is. If we isolate these two doctrines from each other, it is easier for critics to make overly hasty inferences from each one. But when they are taken together, it is harder to do this.

IT MOTIVATES FRUITLESS SEARCHING: 'A GREATER-GOOD THEODICY CONSIGNS US TO A LIFETIME OF FRUITLESS SEARCHING FOR THIS "GREATER GOOD."'

It is sometimes said that the Greater-Good theodicy is pastorally cruel to those who suffer. If we tell them that God has ordained their suffering for a greater good, then we are consigning them to a lifetime of trying to figure out *what* that greater good actually is. But since it hasn't been given them to know this, we are leading them on a wild goose chase, rather than helping them in their suffering. In effect, we are making the problem worse.

This objection is obviously well intended, but it misunderstands what the advocate of the Greater-Good theodicy is actually claiming. It is no part of that theodicy to claim that *we can know*, in any particular instance of suffering, *what is* the greater good aimed at by God in that suffering: what are its features, who will benefit from it, when they will benefit, and so on. We have seen several biblical examples of people *guessing at this and getting it completely wrong*. At most, the Greater-Good theodicy asserts *that* there is a greater good; it does not in addition say that *we can know* what that greater good is in any particular case. The Bible regularly encourages us to trust God even when we cannot figure him out. If anything, appreciating the biblical and philosophical case for the inscrutability of the divine purposes should *free us* from engaging in this fruitless search. This is *never* where God has told us to focus our energies, and so leaving these particular matters with God is the wisest course.

Does the Bible counsel us to yell out on every occasion of suffering, 'It's for the best! It's for the best!' while sticking our fingers in our ears at the cries of those who suffer, thus *increasing* the amount of evil in the world through our insensitivity? Of course not! Like every biblical truth, this truth that God works all things together for good (Rom. 8:28), that our affliction *is* working for us an eternal weight of glory beyond *all* comparison (2 Cor. 4:17), that sometimes it is 'necessary' that we are grieved by various trials (1 Pet. 1:6), must be handled with great thoughtfulness and compassion. Any truth can be abused. But the writers of the Bible did not shrink back from encouraging this perspective, and neither should Christians in their counsels to each other. Those who experience the shock of suffering most likely want our listening ear, our silence, our works of love, and our prayers for God's sustaining grace. At some point when the shock recedes they are usually (though not always!) interested in our answers to difficult questions. Continuing to respect inscrutability because the Bible respects it, while leading them to the God who knows what he is doing, is exactly what the Bible would counsel.

IT IS PASTORALLY COUNTERPRODUCTIVE: '**C**OME ON! **S**AYING THAT **G**OD MERELY ALLOWED THE EVIL, RATHER THAN SAYING HE ENSURED THE EVIL, IS JUST SO MUCH BETTER, PASTORALLY SPEAKING. **Y**OU CANNOT DENY THIS.'

Well, let's see. Let's say a small child is killed in a drive-by shooting. What are the alternatives here, if God has even a modest amount of knowledge and power?

- First response: 'God could have prevented this, but he knew what he was doing by permitting it: working it out to a greater good we should trust him for.'

- Second response: 'God could have prevented this, but some things are more important to God than preventing the death of small children. For instance, the free will of the perpetrator.'

It is certainly not clear (at all!) that the second response is pastorally superior to the first one. The second response gives no hope, no promise, and no assurance that the death was not in vain, whereas the first response encourages faith in a God who not only knows exactly which unfathomable but weighty good he is aiming at, but who is perfectly able to secure it. There is certainly no *moral* difference here: in each case God's decision makes the difference as to whether the death comes to pass. In each case God permits what he could have prevented, and he did so to uphold goods that he took to be *more* valuable than the prolonging of the child's life. This is true whether the good is a particular but inscrutable one God was aiming at, or just the more general good of the value of free will, or the value of moral choices that could possibly flow from free will. 'Your child died because God values the higher-order goods that depend on free will' is no more pastorally comforting than 'Your child died because of the inscrutable providential purpose of God.'

IT DENIES GOD'S GOODNESS: 'I CAN SCARCELY COMPRE-HEND THE IDEA THAT A GOOD GOD WOULD ENSURE THAT EVILS COME TO PASS. THIS IS SIMPLY OUTSIDE WHAT I WOULD REGARD AS EVEN REMOTELY PLAUSIBLE.'

Sometimes we need to have our plausibility judgments challenged by the Bible, though those who do this should always do it with gentleness and respect (1 Pet. 3:15). At the heart of Christianity is the message of the cross, which is a moral evil that God planned to come to pass. This is not a view at the periphery of the Christian faith, but one of its central confessions. It had to be a moral evil, for Jesus had no sins for which he had to suffer, and yet we needed as our substitute one who died the death we sinners ought to have died, who suffered the punishment we ought to have suffered, under judgment and abandoned by God. It is always a moral evil to betray an innocent man to death (as was the case with Judas), and to knowingly put an innocent man to death (as was the case with Pilate). The cross—that is to say, this moral evil—was not some afterthought in the plan of God. God's people are chosen in Christ 'before the foundation of the world' (Eph. 1:4), and 'predestined for adoption as sons through Jesus Christ' (Eph. 1:5).

This book has not directly broached the difficult topic of reconciling divine predestination with human free will. But in a sense, I don't have to. *However* these get reconciled, whatever theory a Christian may have that helps to put these two things together, *any* Christian has to accept what was said in the previous paragraph. But if God can plan one case of freely willed moral evil, ensuring (somehow!) that it does come to pass in his universe for an extraordinarily great good, then what *in principle* prevents him from planning all the rest, also for great goods? The Christian faith doesn't specify how exactly we are to understand the details of predestination and free will. But it *does* specify that the cross was planned by God, and that is enough to make 'planned evil' comprehensible to us. If the critic still balks at this idea, at least we know that it is the central message of Christianity he is rejecting, and not merely one author's attempt to address the problem of evil.

It destroys moral motivation: 'A Greater-Good theodicy would destroy our moral motivation to do good rather than evil.'

If, no matter what we choose, God *will* work it to a greater good, then it doesn't matter *what* we choose! Indeed, even if we choose evil, that will just reveal that such evil was in fact necessary to a greater good. So what's to stop us from choosing evil *every* time? Even if *God* doesn't do evil, the Greater-Good theodicy frees *us* up to do evil that good may come, and it gives us no motivation to do otherwise! So should I do good or evil? It doesn't matter, because God will always work it out 'for the best'. This is a recipe for paralysis in moral decision-making. Any moral motivation to do the right thing is completely undermined.

This is an interesting argument, and some smart philosophers have made it. But the problem is that it *only* draws our attention to the following principle, implicit in Greater-Good theodicy (take 'P' to refer to any person we are contemplating harming):

(1) 'If I were to harm P, then the world would be better off than if I hadn't harmed P.'

This is a true principle, if the Greater-Good theodicy is correct. But restricting our focus to (1) may lead us to overlook a principle that is *also* implied by Greater-Good theodicy:

(2) 'If I were to *refrain* from harming P, then the world would be better off than if I had harmed P.'

Both of these principles would be true in a world governed by the Greater-Good theodicy, but the objection seems to assume that only (1) would be true, that somehow (2) would be excluded. But clearly they would both be true. It's not as if the Greater-Good theodicy envisions God ordering the world in such a way that things are *worse* if I avoid harming people! God works all things for good, not just the bad things. Assuming that both (1) and (2) are true, when I am contemplating my decision *I don't know* which will come to pass: the first part of (1) ('If I were to harm P…') or the first part of (2) ('If I were to refrain from harming P'). I haven't made my decision yet! All I know is that *whichever* of these will come to pass, the rest of the principle will come to pass as well ('… then the world would be better off…'). Knowing this gives me *no* reason to harm P *rather than* not harm him. Remember, I don't know what God has ordained for the greater good. I'm wholly in the dark about this, at the time I make my decision. But then the Greater-Good theodicy doesn't lead me in *either* direction with respect to harming P. These cancel each other out when it comes to motivation, and so any independent reasons I have for thinking that harming P is wrong or blameworthy come into play, and *those* motivations are not undermined by any convictions about divine providence.

This means I have lots of reasons for *not* harming P, and no reason *to* harm P. For instance, perhaps God has told me, in the Ten Commandments (Exod. 20) or in the Sermon on the Mount (Matt. 5–7), not to harm P. Or my parents have reinforced this in my upbringing. Or I can just 'see' by moral intuition that harming P is wrong. None of these reasons for not harming P are undermined by the Greater-Good theodicy at all, and so moral motivation is not undermined. More generally, for all I know, God has ordained the harming of P *or* the not harming of P, and since I don't know which ahead of time, God's ordaining is irrelevant as a practical motivator (or demotivator) as to what I should do.

Maybe if God calls me to be what ethicists call a 'consequentialist' in my moral reasoning, and so wants me to base my moral decision-making on its predicted consequences, on what would lead to the greatest overall good for the world, *then* the idea that 'either way God will work it for good' might somehow paralyze my moral decision-making. But God *hasn't* called me to be a consequentialist, and base my decisions on the sum total of their predicted good consequences. And a good thing too, because I simply don't know how to calculate this! *God* might be in a position to plan the world such that goods are maximized by way of his providential choices, but we certainly are not. We wouldn't have a clue as to how to calculate this. So our moral motivation must come from another corner, as it were, and it is not surprising that the Bible does not seem to commend to Christians the ethic of consequentialism. So it's no good inferring from God's providential planning with respect to evil to *our* moral paralysis in decision-making. We continue to have lots of motivation to do the right thing, and no reason to do the wrong thing rather than the right thing.[1]

IT TREATS PERSONS AS MEANS: 'DON'T GREATER-GOOD THEODICIES SHARE A WEAKNESS WITH UTILITARIANISM, TREATING PERSONS AS MEANS RATHER THAN AS ENDS?'

Utilitarianism is a consequentialist theory of moral rightness according to which we should always act in such a way that we secure the greatest good for the greatest number of people. This sounds attractive, but utilitarianism allows it to be morally right that one person benefits at the expense of another (as long as it leads to the greatest amount of goods). For instance, it might end up being 'moral' to liquidate an entire minority because it will lead to social peace, or to

---

1   Notice that when Paul in Romans 3:5–8 considers the question of whether we should 'do evil that good may come?' he doesn't deny the doctrine that led to the question. He doesn't deny that our unrighteousness is a means of showing God's righteousness, or deny that our lying is a means for God's truth to abound to his glory. Rather, he denies that consequentialism gives us moral motivation at all!

murder someone to save half the tribe. In both cases, people are killed simply as a means to an end, a result that offends our moral sensibilities. In the same way, it seems that on the Greater-Good theodicy, *other* people suffer so that *I* can do a good thing, such as showing sympathy towards their suffering, compassion towards their need, patience toward their sickness, and so on. So one person benefits at another's expense. Is *any* evil permissible, as long as it ensures a greater good? Surely there are limits here.

One reply is to point out that, from a Christian point of view, it is *obvious* that God uses people as means to his ends. This is seemingly related to the right of the potter over the clay (Rom. 9:20–23). Thus: 'The LORD has made everything for its purpose, even the wicked for the day of trouble' (Prov. 16:4). God raised up Pharaoh as a means to an end, so that God might display his power in Pharaoh and proclaim God's name in all the earth (Rom. 9:17; cf. Exod. 9:16). God raises up the Assyrian army to be an 'axe' that he 'hews' with, a 'saw' that he 'wields,' a 'rod' and a 'staff' that he 'lifts,' so that their warmongering would be 'the rod of my anger' against the disobedient Israelites, so that 'the staff in their hands is my fury' (Isa. 10:5, 15). But then God turns around and judges the very rod he raised up (Isa. 10:12). Even 'the Son of Man goes as it has been determined,' and Judas is the means for this in God's plan, 'but woe to that man by whom he is betrayed!' (Luke 22:22).

According to Romans 11:36, all things are not only from God and through God, but *for* God. So nothing that occurs in God's universe is *ultimately* for us, even when it *is* for us. This means that each thing in God's universe is already a means, a means to God's glory. In addition, God could hardly work all things together for good, including the kinds of sufferings mentioned in Romans 8, unless he used the sinful choices of men to bring about that good (these are included in the 'all things'). But in using their choices, he is using *them*, as means to bring about the good. And how could Paul's affliction be preparing for him 'an eternal weight of glory beyond all comparison' (2 Cor. 4:17), unless God was *using* the affliction—and therefore the afflicters— to sanctify and fit Paul for heaven?

Still, it doesn't follow from any of this that God *merely* uses us as means, and perhaps that is what the objector is most worried about. For all we know, if he uses us as means, he aims at goods *for us* as well as at other goods that aren't for us, and there is even a threshold of goods *for us* that he meets in each and every case. But all of that is entirely compatible with God's using us and others for the greater good, including the pains and sufferings we experience.

IT MAKES US MORAL SKEPTICS: 'STRESSING THE INSCRUTA-BILITY OF GOD'S JUSTIFYING REASONS WOULD TURN US INTO MORAL SKEPTICS, ROBBING US OF THE ABILITY TO JUDGE THAT *ANYONE* IS IN THE WRONG. AND THAT'S ABSURD!'

If, 'for all we know,' God has a morally justifying reason for permitting just *any* pain and suffering we observe in the world, then why isn't it the case that, 'for all we know,' any *human being* could have a similarly justifying reason for the suffering *he* brings about? Doesn't this approach to the problem of evil imply, for instance, that we could never convict a human being of a crime in a court of law? The defense lawyer could always say, 'Your honor, for all anyone knows, my client has a perfectly good reason for doing what he did, and your inability to discern that reason is no reason to think he *doesn't* have such a reason!'

Thus, this objection maintains that stressing the divine inscrutability saddles us with a general skepticism about all moral judgments whatsoever. We would have to refrain from judging that *anyone* is in the wrong for bringing about suffering. And that seems to be the end of the criminal justice system, not to mention interpersonal relationships. ('I know you're inflicting lots of pain on me right now, but for all I know you have a good reason, so by all means continue!')

Well, it is understandable that someone would worry about this. And again, some very smart philosophers have voiced this objection. But fortunately, what was argued in chapter 4 was a case for *local* skepticism with respect to a particular territory in which we lack expertise (namely, long-range divine purposes, and necessary connections between present evils and deep goods only realizable by those evils). This is far different from a *global* skepticism that includes all territories whatsoever, including particular territories in which we *do* have expertise (namely, about what motives would suggest themselves to our fellow humans for their choices). We are humans, and we are intimately familiar with the kinds of justifications that humans have for the things they do. So our inferences here about humans are reliable; 'human-sized' reasons are discernible by us, as it were. But we are not God, and so we are not intimately familiar with the full range of complex, deep goods that would be discernible *by God*. Nor are we familiar with all of the necessary connections in the universe that God could exploit to realize these complex, deep goods by way of suffering. Nor do we have in our possession the kind of power that it would take to realize such ends by such means. (But we know at least that *humans* don't have it!) So there is nothing in the argument presented in chapter 4 which would lead us to extend the skepticism beyond the territories knowable only by divine expertise.

Notice that the various 'analogies' for our cognitive limitations (perceptual, scientific, moral, linguistic, aesthetic, and parental), canvassed in chapter 4, all stressed limits to our abilities to discern things in particular areas where we lack expertise. But one doesn't have to be a quantum physicist to be familiar with the kinds of justifications that are accessible to (and therefore employable by) human beings.

IT PROMOTES DIVINE HIDDENNESS: '**T**HE INSCRUTABILITY APPROACH SEEMS BOGUS—WHY DOESN'T **G**OD JUST *TELL US* HIS REASON FOR ALL THE PARTICULAR EVILS IN THE WORLD? **W**HY WOULD HE HIDE HIMSELF IN THIS WAY?'

Perhaps we don't know what we are asking for. On the Greater-Good theodicy, there is no reason to think that just *one* reason applies to every evil. For all we know, there is an unimaginably large number of quite complicated reasons. How much does God have to divulge, in order for the revelation to be satisfactory? (And why would *that* quantity be the threshold?) Beyond this, as we saw in chapter 4, perhaps the reason is so complicated that we wouldn't understand it even if God told us. Do we have an argument that this is *not* the case?

Finally, even assuming that God's reason might be comprehensible to us, one could understand God's unwillingness to tell it to us as just another version of the problem of evil, and so it can be handled in the same way. In other words, this isn't an objection to our solution to the problem of evil, but an invitation to apply the solution all over again. To be sure, God's unwillingness to answer all of our questions in the ways we would prefer no doubt ensures some additional pain and suffering for us. But this is no reason to think that God *doesn't* have a good reason for doing this.

IT'S AN APOLOGETIC COP-OUT: 'ISN'T THE INSCRUTABILITY APPROACH A "COP-OUT" OF CHRISTIAN APOLOGETIC RESPONSIBILITY? PEOPLE NEED ANSWERS, AND YOU GIVE THEM YOUR IGNORANCE.'

Well, that's not exactly fair. I haven't *merely* given them my ignorance! Quite a bit of this book has been devoted to expounding substantial things that the Bible says about God's relation to the evils in the world. It's not question marks all the way down. (Consider chapters 2 and 3 for a review.)

But is the inscrutability perspective defended in chapter 4 a cop-out? That all depends. What *are* the responsibilities of Christians here? Well, what are our responsibilities more generally as human beings, when people ask us questions? If we lack relevant expertise in the area being asked about, is it a cop-out to say—with respect to that particular area—'I don't know'? Why think that? If Christians are *supposed* to know these things, well OK, but again, why think that? There is simply no biblical passage, and no good philosophical reason, that supports the view that Christians should be able to give God's reasons for evils in particular cases.

MAYBE THINGS AREN'T FOR THE BEST: 'THE INSCRUTA-BILITY APPROACH SAYS THAT "FOR ALL WE KNOW" EVILS LEAD TO GREATER GOODS, BUT WHY CAN'T IT BE "FOR ALL WE KNOW" EVILS LEAD TO WORSE EVILS?'

Sure. The point is that we, on our own, cannot make reliable inferences in *either* direction. The appeal to divine inscrutability is not meant to arbitrarily privilege one kind of inference ('evils must lead to goods!') at the expense of another ('evils must lead to evils!'). We don't know enough to come to either of these conclusions on our own. But the appeal to divine inscrutability isn't asking us to come to these kinds of conclusions on our own. We aren't suited to make them. If the critic is interested, the Christian conviction that evils do lead to greater goods is grounded in something else entirely: in divine revelation (in the kinds of passages surveyed in chapters 2 and 3), rather than in our alleged cognitive ability to figure this out just by examining the creation alone.

The point of the inscrutability approach in chapter 4 isn't to argue *for* the Christian conviction with the naked eye, but to undermine the critic's assumption about God's likely reasons for evil, and one doesn't need to appeal to the Bible to do *that*. Premise 2 of the problem of evil says that God would prevent all the evils he could prevent, but that premise assumes he *doesn't* have good reason to permit them.

How does the critic know this? He seems to be claiming knowledge about the emptiness of a territory with which he is not familiar, indeed *could not* be familiar. It's a bonus for Christians that diagnosing this particular cognitive limitation doesn't depend on new-fangled philosophy, but is as old-fangled as the story of Job. The way of theodicy is the way of the fool, if you insist on ruling it in *or* ruling it out, and the way of the wise is to know this.

Conclusion

It is time to draw this book to a close. I have sought to clarify important aspects of (what I take to be) the Christian perspective on evil and suffering, in a way that reminds the *critic* of his burden of proof in raising the problem of evil, and that helps to discharge the *Christian's* burden to make a response.

Speaking for a moment now to my fellow Christians who may be reading this book: it is important for Christians to remember that it is the cross of Christ which unites us, and it is the cross of Christ we proclaim as God's solution for our own personal evils. In the cross our greatest possible need is met: our need for redemption from sin, forgiveness for our offenses, and transformation of life. But the cross of Christ also bears witness to God's willingness to suffer excruciating pain as a man in order to bring us the deepest blessings of his love, a good which is greater than any pain we may suffer. Here the suffering of a Job and a Joseph are but anticipations of the sufferings of Jesus, who glimpsed something of the divine will in his deepest anguish as a human: 'My Father, if it be possible, let this cup pass from me; nevertheless, not as I will, but as you will' (Matt. 26:39). If we fail to preach this Jesus, his suffering will remain inscrutable to the rest of the world, but if we do preach it, God's great and gracious purpose for the world by way of this evil will be known, and eternal blessing will be had by faith (John 3:16).

I speak now to any critics of the Christian faith who may be reading. Whether or not you are convinced by what I say in this book—and I hope and pray that many critics will be convinced!—it is important to clearly lay out the alternatives. A world without God would generate an even worse, because intractable, problem of evil. We would be ultimately alone in our suffering. We would have no hope for eternal fellowship with the Highest Good of existence. The moral intuitions we deeply cherish and by which we seek to live would be pure fantasy, connecting up with no objective obligations in a pitiless, impersonal universe that is utterly indifferent to our pain and the pains of others. Every good as well as every evil would be *ultimately* pointless. We would have no reason to endure in the midst of pain. Life would be lived in bad faith, a series of largely superficial amusements meant to stave off suicide.

For a critic to press 'the problem of evil' against the existence of God would be to use the phenomenon of evil to make the problem of evil *worse* in these and many other ways. It strikes me as a fundamentally irrational act. Should not the critic rather recognize evil as an indication that something is deeply wrong with the universe, that the world is not as it *ought* to be? But if the world has no creator, no providential sustainer, and no judge, why think there *is* a way it 'ought to be'? Interestingly enough, the problem of evil uses moral standards to argue against God, whereas the moral argument for God's existence uses moral standards to argue for God. Is not the critic's struggle with the problem of evil, to the extent that the struggle is deeply existential and not superficial, a witness to the moral standards that are deeply embedded in his outlook? Whence this voice of conscience? I suspect that the problem of evil is an evil that God has worked for good in the lives of many (including me, when I was an unbeliever). It brings them face to face with the voice of the God who has haunted them from the beginning.

Summary of main points

- This book has defended the view that God is the sovereign creator and providential sustainer of the world who, without committing any sins, ensures that natural and moral evils come to pass as necessary means for bringing about great goods that outweigh those evils.

- There are a number of objections to this 'Greater-Good theodicy': (1) it motivates fruitless searching, (2) it's pastorally counter-productive, (3) it denies God's goodness, (4) it destroys moral motivation, (5) it treats persons as means, (6) it makes us moral skeptics, (7) it promotes divine hiddenness, (8) it's an apologetic cop-out, and (9) it allows the view that things aren't for the best.

- Each of these objections can be answered, as long as the doctrines of divine sovereignty and inscrutability are considered together, rather than isolated from one another.

- A world without God would generate an even worse, because intractable, problem of evil.

Appendix

Going Beyond Job, Joseph, and Jesus for the Greater-Good Theodicy

In chapter 2 ('The Greater-Good theodicy: a threefold argument for three biblical themes'), the narratives pertaining to Job, Joseph, and Jesus took center stage. Space did not permit extended reflection on several *other* passages which also seem to weave together the three themes considered in that chapter (the goodness of God's purpose, the sovereignty of God's providence, and the inscrutability of God's ways). These passages include Romans chapter 11, Matthew 4:1–11, and Romans 8:28.

Romans 11

According to what the apostle Paul teaches in Romans chapter 11, the evil of Jewish apostasy—the widespread failure of first-century Jews to place their faith in Jesus, God's 'anointed one' or promised Messiah—is an evil that

God intends for a greater good, one unknown even by Paul except for God's revealing it to him (Rom. 11:33–35). Here God *aims at a great good*: the salvation of the Gentiles (i.e., non-Jews), and ultimately the salvation of the Jews. But he intends this great good to come about *by way of various evils*: the rejection of Jesus by the Jews opens the way to the Gentiles flooding in to the church, and this in turn stirs the Jews up to jealousy so that they will repent as well (Rom.11:11–32). The sovereignty of God in so ordering these goods by these evils is stressed in Romans 11:36. At the same time, God leaves various humans *in the dark* that this is indeed his reason for the evils. By stressing the divine inscrutability in this context (Rom. 11:33–35), Paul implies that he would know nothing of this divine plan unless it had been revealed to him by God. And certainly the unbelieving Jews, in their refusal to accept Jesus as the Messiah, had no inkling of how God would turn their evil to good. (Notice that there is much pain and suffering involved in their apostasy, since their subsequent opposition to the Christian message meant painful persecution of Christians.)

MATTHEW 4:1-11

Or again, the gospel writers teach that the evil of Jesus's being tempted by Satan (Matt. 4:2–11) was both purposed by God the Holy Spirit (Matt. 4:1) and a crucial ingredient in Jesus's living a perfectly righteous life, thus fitting him to be our perfect substitute upon the cross (Heb. 2:10; 5:7–10), and a perfect help in time of need (Heb. 2:18; 4:15–16). Here God *aims at a great good*: Jesus's perseverance in the midst of temptation. God intends that great good to come about *by way of Satan's evil solicitations* to Jesus that he sin. At the same time God leaves humans *in the dark* that this is his reason for the evils—discerning that this was God's method is something that would have been undiscoverable by anyone 'on the scene'. (We only know of God's intention by way of special divine revelation. And just to be clear, *Satan* is the tempter here [Matt. 4:1, 3, 5–6, 8–9], not God [James 1:13]!)

Romans 8:28

Finally, there is a more general passage in the Bible that has often been discussed with respect to the Greater-Good theodicy, since at first glance it seems like a clear endorsement of it. According to Romans 8:28, 'we know that for those who love God all things work together for good, for those who are called according to his purpose.' The phrase 'all things for good' seems to be quite sweeping in its implications. Not a few things, not most things, but all things are worked by God for good, at least for the good of Christians ('for those who love God,' 'for those who are called according to his purpose'). In the preceding context, Paul has been talking about some pretty negative things: 'we suffer with him' (8:17), 'the sufferings of this present time' (8:18), 'futility' (8:20), 'bondage to corruption' (8:21), 'groaning in the pains of childbirth' (8:22), 'our weakness' (8:26). He will immediately go on to speak of such things as 'tribulation, or distress, or persecution, or famine, or nakedness, or danger, or sword' (8:35), during which God will ensure that 'we are more than conquerors through him who loved us' (8:37). It is hard to make the case that the 'all things' of Romans 8:28 doesn't include the very things Paul mentions just prior to and after this verse, and therefore every conceivable suffering a Christian could face!

It is tempting to lessen in some way the force of Paul's statement in Romans 8:28. Perhaps God is working 'in all things' in order to get some good out of them (and this includes our sufferings), but there is no *guarantee* that he will get any good for us by his sincere efforts. But it should be noted that the Greek word for 'in' (as in, God merely works *in* all things for good, rather than actually *working* all things together for good) isn't in the text. We have an action ('works together'), an implied subject for that action (God), an object for that action ('all things'), and a result of the action ('for good'). So good *is* the result of God working together all things.

Beyond this, it seems strange to think that suffering Christians would be comforted by the thought that God has good but *ineffectual* intentions on our behalf, that we would benefit from knowing he sympathizes with our plight but cannot really do anything about it except attempt the best and hope it succeeds. On this view, would we be 'more than conquerors' (Rom. 8:37), or barely survivors? Certainly, the immediately following verses commend the view that God has a plan for his children that stretches from eternity to eternity (8:29–30). This plan is so certain of its execution that its every phase can be spoken of in the past tense. It is a plan the certainty of which is therefore the *reason* we can think that all things—from his foreknowing us in eternity to his glorifying us in heaven—will in fact work for our good.

And in any event, do not the cases of Job, Joseph, and Jesus lead us to think that no evil will stand in the way of God fulfilling his good purpose? In each of these cases God aimed at great goods *and obtained them*. In another letter, Paul assured his readers that his own suffering—things like being 'afflicted,' 'persecuted,' 'struck down,' 'being given over to death'—'is preparing for us an eternal weight of glory beyond all comparison' (2 Cor. 4:17). For Paul, he didn't merely *hope* it would turn out this way, or *speculate* it would turn out this way, or *feel* that it would probably turn out this way. He *knew* his affliction *was* working out to a good beyond all comparison! For all these reasons it is preferable to take Romans 8:28 as teaching that God actually works all things for good, rather than as teaching that God merely works in all things for good (without guaranteeing that the intended good comes to pass).

Suggested Further Reading

- William P. Alston, 'The Inductive Argument from Evil and the Human Cognitive Condition', reprinted in Daniel Howard-Snyder (ed.), *The Evidential Argument From Evil* (Indiana University Press, 1996), pp. 97–125.
- Alistair Begg, *The Hand of God: Finding His Care in All Circumstances* (Moody, 2001).
- Jerry Bridges, *Trusting God* (NavPress, 1988).
- John Calvin, *Institutes of the Christian Religion*, I, chapters 16–18.
- D. A. Carson, *How Long, O Lord?* (2nd edn.) (Baker, 2006).
- John M. Frame, *Apologetics: A Justification of Christian Belief* (P&R, 2015), chapters 7–8.
- Paul Helm, *The Providence of God* (IVP, 1994), chapters 7–8.

- Daniel Howard-Snyder, 'God, Evil, and Suffering', chapter 4 of Michael J. Murray (ed.), *Reason for the Hope Within* (Eerdmans, 1999).
- C. S. Lewis, *The Problem of Pain* (Macmillan, 1962).
- John Piper and Justin Taylor (eds), *Suffering and the Sovereignty of God* (Crossway, 2006).
- Alvin Plantinga, *Warranted Christian Belief* (Oxford University Press, 2000), chapter 14.
- Richard Swinburne, *Providence and the Problem of Evil* (Oxford University Press, 1998).

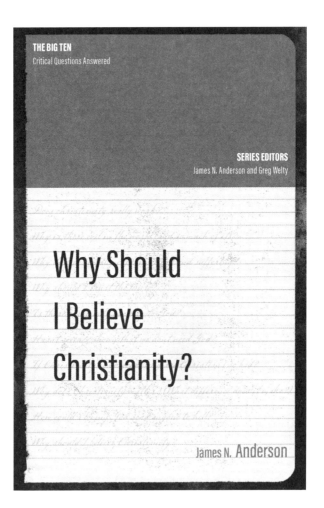

ISBN 978-1-7819-1869-2

Why Should I Believe Christianity?

James N. Anderson

Some people boldly claim, 'Christianity is fine for some, but it isn't for me'. Others feel it is just outdated and irrelevant. For better or worse, everyone in the Western world has come into contact with Christianity: we all have some opinion on it.

James N. Anderson, with a clear, humorous logic, explores what Christianity really claims, and shows the underlying reason and consistency behind these claims. By the end of *Why Should I Believe Christianity?*, while you may not agree with the Christian worldview, it is impossible to be left sitting on the fence.

... The Christian ministry, taken as a whole, must be understood as an apologetic calling. This is why books like Why Should I Believe Christianity? *deserve careful reading by pastors and laypeople alike. In this book, believers will find a compelling defense of the Christian worldview and the resources necessary to stand firm in a faithless age.*

Albert Mohler

President, The Southern Baptist Theological Seminary,
Louisville, Kentucky

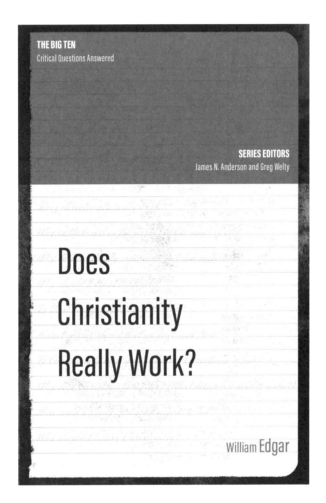

THE BIG TEN
Critical Questions Answered

SERIES EDITORS
James N. Anderson and Greg Welty

Does
Christianity
Really Work?

William Edgar

ISBN 978-1-7819-1775-6

Does Christianity Really Work?

William Edgar

Wasn't the South African Apartheid supported by Christians? Weren't the Crusades motivated by greed, but advocated by the church? Don't phoney television preachers manipulate viewers into donating money? William Edgar addresses these and other questions honestly, without attempting to dismiss or explain away their uncomfortable realities. He displays the good aspects of the church even more brilliantly through frankly and Biblically acknowledging the bad. If you have ever asked the question *Does Christianity Really Work?* this will be an interesting and enlightening read, whatever your prior convictions.

Edgar approaches difficult questions with pastoral care and theological wisdom. He acknowledges the ongoing reality of sin as the reason behind personal and corporate failure. He also points out the many instances of good accomplished by those with an explicitly Christian worldview—the abolition of slavery, health care, women's rights, art, music, social reform and much much more …. This book would be great to hand out to friends who were perhaps interested but skeptical about the claims of Christianity and the record of Christians.

Evangelicals Now

Also available from Christian Focus
Publications …

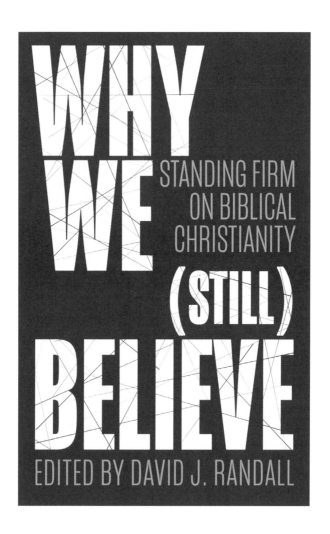

ISBN 978-1-5271-0088-6

Why We (Still) Believe
Standing Firm on Biblical Christianity

DAVID J. RANDALL (ED.)

The West has become permeated with a culture that doesn't 'do' God. Many people assert that we have progressed, while Christians are still clinging to out-dated ideas. In *Why We (Still) Believe*, fourteen contributors focus on several specific contemporary attacks on Christianity, showing why they 'continue in the faith' (Col.1:23).

Contributors: Andy Bannister, Iver Martin, John Ellis, Vince Vitale, Maher Samuel, John Blanchard, Joe Barnard, David J. Randall, Stefan Gustavsson, Richard Lucas, David Robertson, Nola Leach, Gordon MacDonald, (the late) Gordon Wilson.

In a confused culture and an uncertain church, we urgently need this brave and confident clarion call. Confronting the increasingly strident challenges to faith, this is a stimulating, robust and timely response.

Jonathan Lamb
Keswick Ministries, CEO and minister-at-large

ISBN 978-1-7819-1710-7

God—Is He Out There?

Mez McConnell

If God exists, prove it then! If God exists, what does it have to do with me? If all this is true, now what? This series of short workbooks, from the 9 Marks Urban series, are designed to help you think through some of life's big questions. It all starts with the most important question of all: God—Is He Out There? The questions that follow all hinge on our answer to that question. If we answer that there is a God, then how can we get to know Him and how should we now live?

A life committed to following Jesus isn't easy, so we need all the help we can get! I'm thankful, then, for a resource like this. In God—Is He Out There? *Mez McConnell tackles the difficult—yet central—questions of Christian theology in a way that is accessible, practical, and personal.*

Jared C. Wilson

Director of Content Strategy for Midwestern Baptist Theological Seminary and Managing Editor of For The Church, Midwestern's site for gospel-centered resources

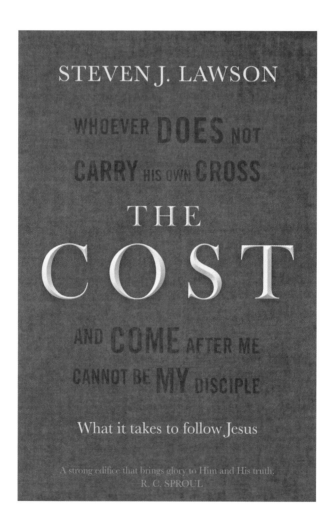

STEVEN J. LAWSON

WHOEVER **DOES** NOT
CARRY HIS OWN CROSS

THE
COST

AND **COME** AFTER ME
CANNOT BE **MY** DISCIPLE

What it takes to follow Jesus

A strong edifice that brings glory to Him and His truth.
R. C. SPROUL

ISBN 978-1-7819-1955-2

The Cost

What it takes to follow Jesus

Steven J. Lawson

Nestled in a few verses in Luke's Gospel is a Jesus who would not have been tolerated today: He was not politically correct and He certainly did not try to save people's feelings. Steven J. Lawson unpacks these few verses, looking at the unashamed honesty, passion, and urgency with which Jesus explains the life-long cost involved in choosing to follow Him. True Christianity is the biggest sacrifice any person ever makes ... but it is in pursuit of the most precious prize ever glimpsed.

Like a master builder Steve Lawson gives us the foundation of Jesus' own words to erect a frame showing the cost, demands, gains and losses of following Christ. In doing so, Dr. Lawson gives us a strong and firm edifice that brings glory to Him and His truth.

R. C. Sproul

Founder & Chairman of Ligonier Ministries, Orlando

Christian Focus Publications

Our mission statement –

STAYING FAITHFUL

In dependence upon God we seek to impact the world through literature faithful to His infallible Word, the Bible. Our aim is to ensure that the Lord Jesus Christ is presented as the only hope to obtain forgiveness of sin, live a useful life and look forward to heaven with Him.

Our books are published in four imprints:

CHRISTIAN
FOCUS

CHRISTIAN
HERITAGE

Popular works including bio-graphies, commentaries, basic doctrine and Christian living.

Books representing some of the best material from the rich heri-tage of the church.

MENTOR

CF4•K

Books written at a level suitable for Bible College and seminary students, pastors, and other seri-ous readers. The imprint includes commentaries, doctrinal studies, examination of current issues and church history.

Children's books for quality Bible teaching and for all age groups: Sunday school curriculum, puzzle and activity books; personal and fam-ily devotional titles, biographies and inspirational stories – because you are never too young to know Jesus!

Christian Focus Publications Ltd,
Geanies House, Fearn, Ross-shire,
IV20 1TW, Scotland, United Kingdom.
www.christianfocus.com